Sylvia Henry gave

to Ruth Calkins.
Wesley Terrace 537.

ISAIAH SPEAKS

Isaiah Speaks

S. Paul Schilling

Woman's Division of Christian Service
Board of Missions of The Methodist Church

Woman's Division of Christian Service
Board of Missions of The Methodist Church
New York, N. Y.

Picture on Cover:	Michelangelo: *Isaiah*, Sistine Chapel (detail)
Scroll Inside Front Cover:	Book of Isaiah, c. 100 B.C. From the Dead Sea Scrolls
Map Inside Back Cover:	Palestine in time of Isaiah
Cover Design and Book Format:	Claire Valentine

CONTENTS

CONTENTS

Part One

INTRODUCING ISAIAH

I

THE TEACHING
AND THE TESTIMONY

THE IMPORTANCE OF THE BOOK

WITH the possible exception of The Psalms, no
other Old Testament writing has so great a claim
on the attention of Christians as the Book of
Isaiah. In the Christian movement, as in Judaism,
its influence has been profound. Its vivid poetic
imagery, its depth of spiritual insight, its disclosures of religious truth, and its keen ethical
sensitivity make it a rich resource for all who
would learn of God or practice his presence.

THE INFLUENCE OF ISAIAH: All four of the gospel
writers use language taken from Isaiah in introducing John the Baptist as the voice crying in the
wilderness, "Prepare the way of the Lord, make
his paths straight" (Matt. 3:1-3; Mark 1:1-3;
Luke 3:1-6; John 1:19-23; Isa. 40:3). A quotation
from Isaiah 42:1 is used to express God's approval
of Jesus at both his baptism and his transfiguration
(Matt. 3:17; 17:5; Mark 1:11; 9:7; Luke 3:22;

3

9:35). When Jesus visited his home synagogue at Nazareth and there sought to explain the nature of his mission, he read and applied to himself the stirring words of the prophet: "The Spirit of the Lord is upon me . . . " (Isa. 61:1-2; Luke 4:16-30). Many months later he rebuked the money-changers in the temple with a passage from Isaiah: "My house shall be called a house of prayer for all peoples," adding, "But you have made it a den of robbers" (Isa. 56:7; Mark 11:17; Matt. 21:13; Luke 19:46).

These instances are illustrative of the wide use of Isaiah made in the New Testament writings as a whole. The New Testament, all in all, contains 213 quotations from, or allusions to, this one Old Testament book. Undoubtedly the most significant ones are those which conceive the messianic role of Jesus not as that of the nationalistic Son of David or the apocalyptic Son of man, but in terms of the inspired suffering servant passages of Isaiah (42:1-4; 49:1-6; 50:4-9; 52:13 through 55:12; see Matt. 12:17-21). The importance of this identification for later Christian life and thought can hardly be exaggerated.

The influence of Isaiah, so apparent in the New Testament, is also pronounced in Christian hymnody and other church music. Almost a third of the scriptural text of Handel's "Messiah" is direct quotation from this book. The hymns in *The Methodist Hymnal* contain sixty-five references to passages in Isaiah—more than any other biblical book except The Psalms, Matthew, Luke, and John.

The language, ideas, and insights of Isaiah have thus come to exert a weighty, if often unrecognized, influence on multitudes of worshiping Christians. Attitudes and aspirations expressed in worship have a way of affecting materially the beliefs and conduct of those who utter them.

THE RELEVANCE OF THE BOOK TODAY: Paradoxically, this book, which has been so influential and in some respects so well known, is in other ways one of the least known and understood of biblical writings. The majority of Christians are familiar with chapters 6, 40, and 55, the messianic prophecies, and the servant poems, but with little else. This is due partly to the fact that many of the most meaningful passages cannot be understood without acquaintance with the specific historical circumstances which called them forth. Such acquaintance often requires extra-biblical study for which the ordinary reader has either little opportunity or small inclination.

Yet the historical situations are so similar to some of those characteristic of the twentieth century that the messages called forth by them have an astonishing contemporary relevance. The territory covered by any newspaper map of the Middle East, so strategically important today, is almost identical with that which formed the setting for the prophecies of Isaiah. The names of the countries occupying it are partly the same, partly different, but now as then the area is the scene of an economic and political power-struggle complicated by religious rivalries. Now as then, in the Middle East and around the world, men are reaping the bitter fruits of self-centered pride, greed, indifference to human need, and disregard for the righteous will of a universal God.

Through the prophet's words, therefore, the divine Word speaks to our time almost as revealingly as to his own. We too walk in darkness and the shadow of death, and basically for the same reasons. We too are threatened with exile, not from Palestine but from the earth itself. We desperately need the light of which Isaiah so eloquently speaks. To ignore that light would be inexpressibly foolish. To place ourselves where its rays may illuminate our path is the counsel of true wisdom, whatever the effort may cost.

THE AUTHENTICITY OF THE TEXT: Thanks to the amazing discoveries of ancient scrolls recently made in caves near the Dead Sea, we can turn to the book itself with exceptional confidence in the accuracy and authenticity of its text. The manuscript of Isaiah found in 1947, and now owned by St. Mark's Monastery in Jerusalem, is the only Dead Sea Scroll to contain a complete biblical book.[1] It is also the oldest of the scrolls, dating from about the second century B. C. Since the oldest previously known manuscript of Isaiah dates from the ninth century A. D., the St. Mark's Scroll carries us about 1,000 years closer to the original book. This makes all the more remarkable its substantial agreement with the official Hebrew text.[2]

[1] The other Isaiah scroll, owned by Hebrew University, contains only part of chapters 10 through 66. An excellent work on the scrolls is Millar Burrows, *The Dead Sea Scrolls* (New York: Viking Press, 1955).

There are a good many minor variations, and some of them acquaint us with more ancient readings and shed valuable light on uncertain passages. Yet the scholars who prepared the Revised Standard Version of the Old Testament actually adopted, after careful study, only thirteen readings where the scroll departs from the traditional text. Our Book of Isaiah is a translation from essentially the same book from which Jesus read when he arose in the synagogue at Nazareth.

THE NATURE OF THE BOOK

A PROPHETIC BOOK: In the Hebrew Scriptures, comprising the Law, the Prophets, and the Writings, Isaiah belongs to the second division, which itself consists of two parts, the Former and the Latter Prophets. The Former Prophets comprise the historical books from Joshua through Kings (except Ruth). The Latter Prophets include Isaiah, Jeremiah, Ezekiel, and the Book of the Twelve—a single volume of so-called Minor Prophets, which are minor in length only and not in significance.

What is prophecy? Basically, it is not prediction but proclamation. *To prophesy is to say or tell forth* ; it is not to speak before events but *to speak for God in the midst of events*. The great literary prophets of the Old Testament were not primarily foretellers of the future but forthtellers of divine truth. They were at once dedicated servants of God and close students of the life of their times. Filled with a sense of divine mission and illuminated by

² Usually designated the Masoretic text, because it was fixed by learned Jews called Masoretes about the eighth century A. D.

7

their firsthand experience of the Most High, they interpreted and declared the will of God for his people.

Inevitably such activity involved some prediction. The prophets correctly perceived that obedience to God's purposes promotes man's highest welfare while disobedience leads to chaos and destruction. They therefore proclaimed sharply what lay ahead if a certain path was followed. They "express their moral certainty and spiritual understanding of *what will be* because of *what is*, because Yahweh and no other god is Lord."[1]

Isaiah is in the truest sense a prophetic book. In a series of critical situations it declares the divine will, and proclaims doom or offers hope for the future in relation to Israel's response to that will.

A COLLECTION OF PROPHECIES: The discerning reader of Isaiah quickly notes its lack of any clear chronological sequence. Similarly, he is impressed by wide variations in style and language, historical background, and religious ideas.

1. There are distinct differences in language and literary style, particularly noticeable in a comparison of chapters 1 through 39 and 40 through 66. The style of the former is direct, concise, concrete, diversified; that of the latter is marked by flowery eloquence, poetic beauty, repetition, and less variety and concreteness. Certain Hebrew words and phrases appear frequently in one part and scarcely at all in the other.

[1]R. B. Y. Scott, *The Relevance of the Prophets* (New York: The Macmillan Co., 1944), p. 14. Used by permission of the publisher.

2. The historical background of chapters 1 through 39 is for the most part clearly that of the eighth century B. C., while chapters 40 through 55 deal with persons and political situations characteristic of the Babylonian exile in the middle of the sixth century. Reading consecutively chapters 35 and 40, omitting the intervening historical narrative, one becomes vividly aware of the vastly different circumstances reflected and the differences in the messages proclaimed. Moreover, even chapters 1 through 39 contain prophecies which suggest exilic as well as post-exilic origins.

3. There are sharp contrasts in religious and theological concepts. The notion of the "remnant"—so prominent in chapters 1-39—is largely missing in 40 through 66. The messianic king of 9:1-6 and 11:1-9 stands in sharp contrast to the suffering servant so movingly portrayed in 40 through 55. Chapters 40 through 55 stress the universal reign of the one God who is the infinite Creator of the ends of the earth, thus voicing ideas which are only implicit in the earlier portions.

Circumstances like these suggest that the book which bears the name of Isaiah is actually the work of a number of authors writing at different times. A century of painstaking research has led overwhelmingly to this conclusion. The book is a collection, indeed a collection of collections, of prophetic oracles, many of them anonymous. They were produced during a period of several hundred years and assembled because of their permanent worth without regard to original authorship or chronological order. The book might indeed be called a miniature prophetic library, covering most of the period of Hebrew prophetic activity.

DIVERSITY IN AUTHORSHIP: It is true that Isaiah the son of Amoz has traditionally been regarded as the author of the entire book. This tradition is based on allusions in the apocryphal writing Ecclesiasticus (48:22-25), various New Testament passages (Matt. 3:3 and parallels; Matt. 8:17; 12:17; Luke 4:17; John 1:23; Acts 8:28; Rom. 10:16, 20), and Josephus' *Antiquities* (XI, 1, sec. 2). However, such references are probably based principally on the title of the canonical book. They identify the source of the material cited without expressing a critical judgment as to authorship or even raising the question. In fact, the use of a name in the title of a book does not necessarily imply that the person named is the writer of the whole work. For example, two Old Testament books bear the name of Samuel, though the record of Samuel's death in I Sam. 25:1 makes plain that he himself could not have written more than the first twenty-four chapters.

Two other things should be borne in mind as we consider the composite character of the Book of Isaiah. First, the truth and value of its religious teachings are unaffected by its authorship. The plays generally attributed to Shakespeare are great literature, whoever wrote them. Their language will be just as beautiful and their understanding of human life just as profound even if some day they should prove to have been written by Christopher Marlowe or Francis Bacon. "O come, all ye faithful" is an authentic expression of Christian worship, even though the name of its Latin author is veiled in mystery. The splendor of the Cathedral of Chartres is undiminished by our ignorance of the names of its architect or the creators of its magnificent stained-glass windows. The lofty affirmations of the majesty and mercy of God in Isaiah 55 are gloriously true, whether written, as they almost certainly were, by an unknown prophet of the Babylonian exile, or by Isaiah.

Secondly, questions of date and authorship, though important and helpful to understanding, are not central. They are the frame of the picture, not the painting itself; the setting of the biblical revelation, not the revelation itself. The conscientious Bible student is free to examine them open-mindedly without exposing himself to the charge that his conclusions are unorthodox or unchristian. It is neither more nor less *religious* to regard the historical Isaiah as the writer of the entire Book of Isaiah than to hold some other view. Issues of this kind must be decided purely on the basis of the best evidence. The sole relevant question is, what are the facts, and what is the best explanation of them? If God is the God of truth, he will approve the answer which grows out of the most humble and thoughtful search for the truth. We are commanded to love God with our *minds* as well as with our hearts.

THE GROWTH OF THE BOOK: How can we account for the extended and rather complicated

11

editorial process which the Book of Isaiah has apparently gone through? How did other materials come to be added to the passages written by Isaiah himself? No one can say with certainty. However, several suggestions may aid our understanding.

1. Isaiah was primarily not a systematic writer, but an orator and statesman who relied mainly on the spoken word. However, he did commit some of his utterances to writing in order to preserve them, and sometimes worked out his ideas with great care, particularly at critical times. The resultant summaries of his oral teaching, originally on separate rolls, were collected by his followers, and possibly supplemented by fragments which had never been publicly uttered. Ultimately these formed the nucleus of the collections comprising the canonical Book of Isaiah. But apparently there was no effort or intent to limit the compilation to the prophecies of Isaiah himself.

2. Hebrew editors seem to have dealt with prophetic oracles much as do modern editors in collecting hymns, though with less interest in accurate data concerning origins. Once satisfied that a writing contained a message from God, they included it with other similar messages with no sense of incongruity. In *The Methodist Hymnal* the opening hymn is Reginald Heber's "Holy, Holy, Holy," published in 1827 after the author's death. It is followed by "Come, Thou Almighty King," an anonymous hymn from about 1757. The third hymn, "Before Jehovah's Awe-full Throne," was

written by Isaac Watts in 1719, though it is really a poetic version of Psalm 100, which was composed by an unknown author probably between 538 and 150 B. C. All three hymns are lofty expressions of praise to God. In spite of uncertainties concerning authorship and wide disparity in times of writing, they seem to belong together, and no one objects to their standing in the hymnal side by side. Biblical editors and copyists were no more hesitant about grouping oracles of different prophets. The conviction that several oracles were alike produced by genuine spokesmen for God, and perhaps broadly similar in point of view, was sufficient reason for combining them in the same scroll.

3. Understanding is gained if we consider the physical nature of the "books" in which the Old Testament writings were preserved. They were composed of pieces of skin or papyrus sewn together in strips of varying length, which were rolled at the ends for convenience in reading and storing. Blank rolls were expensive and not plentiful, and persons who wanted copies of particular writings often used vacant space or partially filled rolls for the purpose. This sometimes brought unrelated materials together on the same roll, somewhat as today miscellaneous musical numbers are sometimes recorded on the same tape or disk. In such cases the original heading, usually the name of the author of the first passage, served to identify the roll in a library of such rolls. In time, the writer so named could easily come to be regarded as the

author of the entire roll, especially if the other authors were unknown.

Thus "Isaiah," which originally specified the author of the initial prophecies in a collection, became in time the label of a roll which also contained various anonymous writings. This process apparently reached completion about 200 B. C., when the prophetic writings then circulating were copied on four papyrus scrolls of approximately equal length. The result was a four-volume edition of the "Latter Prophets," comprising Isaiah, Jeremiah, Ezekiel, and "The Twelve." Jeremiah and Ezekiel are mainly the work of individual prophets, while the other two are anthologies. After the then existing Book of Isaiah—probably chapters 1 through 39 of our canonical book, already an anthology—was copied on the first scroll, the remaining space was used for the anonymous prophecies of chapters 40 through 66, which were then in circulation as a separate document or documents. The heading in Isaiah 1:1 was naturally taken as the title of the entire scroll, and gradually the later as well as the earlier oracles were ascribed to the prophet there named.[1]

UNITY OF SPIRIT: In spite of the evident differences, the prophecies comprising the Book of Isaiah are marked by an underlying unity of spirit which amply justifies their inclusion in the same collection. It would be a gross error to regard the book merely as a catch-all in which completely un-

[1] This reconstruction is suggested by Robert H. Pfeiffer in his *Introduction to the Old Testament* (New York: Harper and Brothers, 1948), p. 415.

related materials were accidentally placed simply because space remained on a roll. Both Isaiah and the author of chapters 40 through 55 speak to the needs of a people in times of political and spiritual crisis, from the vantage point of a sublime faith. Both regard men and nations as under the judgment and providence of God. Both perceive spiritual realities missed by their contemporaries. In fact, Martin Buber believes that the unknown prophet of the exile definitely thinks of himself as a disciple of Isaiah, called to unseal and fulfill the teaching of his predecessor.[1] He is thus with good reason named the Second Isaiah. Most of the prophecies of the book may indeed be products of a movement which stemmed from Isaiah himself, and whose representatives felt themselves to be carrying on his work. At any rate, most of the book breathes his spirit.

OUTLINE OF THE BOOK: It is nevertheless true that the Book of Isaiah can be understood only when the differences cited earlier are accepted at full value. The book then falls naturally into two main sections, chapters 1 through 39 and 40 through 66. Most good commentaries are organized according to this division.

The first section is usually subdivided somewhat as follows:

1 through 12. *Oracles addressed chiefly to Judah,* with some narration, written almost entirely by Isaiah.

[1] Martin Buber, *The Prophetic Faith* (New York: The Macmillan Co. 1949), pp. 202-205.

15

13 through 23. *Prophecies of doom on foreign nations*, some by Isaiah and others by later writers.

24 through 27. *A booklet of late eschatological prophecy*, that is, prophecy dealing with "last things," involving divine judgment and the consummation of the divine purpose.

28 through 33. *A collection of "woe" oracles*, chiefly by Isaiah, with a later appendix of both judgment and promise concerning the age to come.

34 and 35. *Two vivid eschatological prophecies*, post-Isaianic in origin.

36 through 39. *A historical narrative* dealing with Sennacherib's invasion of Judah and Isaiah's relation to it, taken largely from II Kings.

The second section of the book falls naturally into two parts, chapters 40 through 55 and 56 through 66. The former is the work of an unknown poet-prophet who, writing in Babylon about 540 B. C., proclaimed the deliverance of the exiles and the coming redemption of Israel through the action of God. The latter reflects the problems faced by the Jewish community in Jerusalem after the exile: it was probably written by a disciple (or disciples) of Second Isaiah during the century following the return to Palestine.

The three succeeding parts of this book will follow these broad divisions. In the discussion of Isaiah 1 through 39 limitations of space will compel us to confine our attention to the prophecies of Isaiah himself, omitting, for example, any consideration of chapters 24 through 27 and 34 and 35.

Part Two

ISAIAH, CHAPTERS 1-39

II

WHOM SHALL I SEND?

THE TIMES[1]

ISAIAH of Jerusalem lived during one of the most critical and stirring periods of Hebrew history. His prophetic ministry was so intimately related to the political events of his time that we cannot understand his message apart from its historical setting. Born in the middle of the reign of Uzziah, king of Judah (783-742 B.C.), he began his prophetic work in the year of Uzziah's death and carried it on for four or five decades during the reigns of Jotham (742-735 B.C.), Ahaz (735-715 B.C.), and Hezekiah (715-687 B.C.).[2] During this period the dominant world power was Assyria, which was ruled successively by Tiglath-pileser III (745-727 B.C.), Shalmaneser V (727-722 B.C.), Sargon II (722-705 B.C), and Sennacherib (705-681 B.C.).

[1] For the biblical account of the events which form the setting for Isaiah's ministry, see Isa. 36 through 39; II Kings 15:17 through 20:21.

[2] Because of the difficulty of reconciling biblical and other evidence as to the dates of these four kings, authorities differ considerably in their conclusions. The dates listed are those arrived at by William F. Albright and included in the chronology of George A. Barrois in *The Interpreter's Bible* (Nashville: Abingdon Press, 1951-57), I, 146-47.

The foreign policies of most of the eastern Mediterranean nations were motivated above all by the desire to avoid or to overthrow Assyrian rule. For Judah the time was one of ferment and insecurity. During the years of Isaiah's prophetic activity the northern Hebrew kingdom of Israel passed out of existence; invading armies ranged back and forth across Palestine; and Judah herself confronted threat after threat, fell into subjection to Assyria, rebelled, and barely escaped destruction and captivity. Against this turbulent background Isaiah carried on his prophetic activity.

THE MAN

A native of Judah, Isaiah lived most of his life in Jerusalem. He was well educated and embodied the highest culture of his time. His scathing accusations against the ruling classes of the capital city reflect a thorough familiarity with their attitudes and practices. He had ready access to the royal court, and may have belonged to the king's council. His religious utterances dealt repeatedly with problems of government and international relations. He was respected and listened to by kings, even though they usually persisted in the short-sighted policies which he courageously opposed.

But Isaiah was far more than a member of the socially elite. His real aristocracy was of the spirit. From beginning to end he was motivated by a sense of divine mission and strengthened by a power which came from his firsthand experience of the

Most High. The nature of his call and his intimate acquaintance with the architecture and worship of the temple suggest that he may have been a priest In any event, he spoke with the spiritual authority of one who had met God and knew himself to be a spokesman of the Lord.

Isaiah was apparently married about the time of his call, or shortly thereafter, and his deep religious commitment found natural expression in the life of his family. He spoke of his wife as "the prophetess." Even his sons, given symbolic names, became living embodiments of his prophetic message. The elder was called Shear-jashub ("A remnant will return"), and the other Maher-shalal-hashbaz ("Swift the spoiling, prompt the plundering," or "Swift-booty-speedy-prey"). How these "preacher's kids" felt about their rather unwieldy names we do not know, but wherever they went they were effective reminders of central truths proclaimed by their father. Even today children are often given names which reflect the hopes and ideals cherished for them by their parents: Grace, Faith, Theodore or Dorothy (Gift of God), Paula Carol (Little Song). "Isaiah" itself in Hebrew means "Jehovah is salvation," and though it was a fairly common name in ancient Israel, the prophet saw in it a fitting symbol of his ministry.[1]

THE CALL

ISAIAH'S VISION OF GOD: Appropriately, Isaiah's ministry began in a vision of God. He tells us about

[1] It is noteworthy that the names Isaiah, Joshua, Jeshua, Hosea, and Jesus all have the same root.

it in a passage which was probably composed some years after the event, since he is able to look back on "the year that King Uzziah died." It seems likely that in 734, after Ahaz had stubbornly ignored Isaiah's counsel, the prophet collected or wrote down the oracles uttered thus far in his ministry. To these he added, in explanation and validation of his message, the account of his call in chapter six.

Those who recall the sobering impact on the American people of the death of President Roosevelt in 1945 can imagine something of the anxiety with which the people of Judah contemplated the death of one who had been their king for more than forty years. Whether Uzziah had already died or was reaching the final stages of his long illness we do not know, but the time of Isaiah's vision marked the end of an era. After a period of great prosperity, storm-clouds were gathering, and vague fears made heavy the hearts of the people. Yet sensitive souls frequently see more clearly in times of darkness than when all is bright. I sometimes gaze at night from my study window at the lights in the town below. They always shine more clearly and beautifully when the room itself is dark. Even so, as Isaiah in the darkness peered into the unknown future, *he saw God, and in the light of God he saw himself and his nation more truly than ever before.*

Probably Isaiah was actually in the temple at Jerusalem, perhaps participating officially in some important religious festival, when he experienced his ecstatic vision. Psychologically, it was an intense spiritual experience with vivid auditory and visual accompaniments. But for Isaiah the vision and the insights it brought were far more than the consequences of an overwrought emotional state; they were rather the work of the Lord himself in whose temple he was worshiping. Hebrew and Christian faith concur in this judgment.

The overwhelming impression made on Isaiah by his experience was that of the awesome holiness of God. Standing perhaps in the doorway "between the vestibule and the altar" (Joel 2:17), he "saw the Lord sitting upon a throne, high and lifted up," with the skirts of his royal robe filling the temple. Attending the heavenly King were the seraphim, unearthly, superhuman beings whose very name, meaning fiery or burning ones, suggests the blinding splendor of the ineffable God whom they served. Each had six wings; with two he covered his face lest he look on the face of God, with two he covered his own body, and with two he flew. The seraphim called to one another:

Holy, Holy, Holy is the LORD of hosts;
the whole earth is full of his glory.

But words, even thrice repeated, could not proclaim fittingly the exalted perfection of the Eternal. As though in answer to the adoring cries of the winged creatures, the foundations of the doorway shook, and the temple was filled with smoke, a symbol which had signified the presence of the Lord since the days of Moses at Sinai. Isaiah stood transfixed by these manifestations of the sovereign grandeur of God, revealed here as King, not of Judah only, but of the whole world.

Standing thus before the Most High, the prophet inevitably felt his own unworthiness. In sheer contrast with the divine holiness, he was shaken by the consciousness of his personal sin and his involvement in the sin of his people. "Woe is me! for I am lost; for I am a man of unclean lips, and I dwell in the midst of a people of unclean lips." Still another thought alarmed him: "for my eyes have seen the King, the LORD of hosts." According to Hebrew tradition, no man could look at the face of God and live (Exod. 33:20).

Soon, however, the lost was found. One of the seraphim flew to him with a glowing stone taken with tongs from the altar, touched his mouth with it, and said, "Your guilt is taken away, and your sin is forgiven." The Hebrew makes plain that the "burning coal" was not a glowing ember, but the type of heated hearthstone that was used for baking in Hebrew homes. Symbolically, the stone from the altar brought the repentant man into contact with the divine holiness, removing his defilement as fire cleanses and purifies. At the same time, the whole act made unmistakably plain the forgiveness of God.

The resultant transformation affected not only Isaiah's lips, but his whole being. When the Lord, taking counsel with the assembled company, asked, "Whom shall I send, and who will go for us?" Isaiah replied, in unhesitating obedience, "Here am I! Send me." Led by his vision of God to a consciousness of sin and an assurance of forgiveness, he responded with the dedication of his life.

The prophet's commission followed quickly, but it was not an inspiring one. Indeed, it might easily have tempted a less consecrated soul to reconsider his response. He was to declare to "this people" a message of doom, which instead of producing repentance would make them even more stubbornly rebellious. We can readily imagine the puzzlement of his heart as he asked, "How long, O Lord?" only to be told to carry on until the land was desolate and its people in exile. The text of verse 13 is obscure, and it may be a very late modification of Isaiah's original message of complete doom. Its absence from the Septuagint[1] suggests that it was missing from the Hebrew scroll from which this Greek translation was made about 150 B.C. The survival of a tenth is inconsistent with the complete depopulation pictured in verses 11-12, though harmonious with the idea of the remnant elsewhere proclaimed by Isaiah.

Verse 10 should be taken idiomatically rather than literally. In the command to dull the minds of the people ("make the heart fat," and "shut their eyes,") the imperative form is used to state the realistic expectation that they will actually deepen their opposition rather than accept the divine will; and the words, "lest they see" (that they may not see) make explicit the expected *result* of the prophetic proclamation rather than the *purpose*

[1] So called because the work of translating the Old Testament into Greek was done by about seventy Alexandrian scholars.

of it. The passage really expresses a demonstrable psychological fact—that obstinate, proud, sinful unbelief in spiritual truth is often heightened rather than diminished by the fuller disclosure of that truth, and that minds which repeatedly reject what they hear finally become immune to it. "This is the judgment, that the light has come into the world, and men loved darkness rather than light, because their deeds were evil" (John 3:19).

It is clear that Isaiah began his prophetic work under no illusions as to its outcome. Though the wording of his commission may be colored somewhat by his later experience with the obstinate Ahaz, there is no evidence that he ever cherished optimistic expectations of success. As George Adam Smith has written, verses 9-13 are "only a forcible anticipation of the prophet's actual experience."[1]

The true prophet is not influenced by calculations of possible success or failure. Under an inward constraint, he speaks the divine word that is given to him; like Luther at Worms, he can do no other. Such was the case with Isaiah. The voice of the Lord said to him in effect, "Declare to Judah the destruction that is certain if her people do not turn from their evil ways. They will not change, but preach my word anyway." Isaiah did.

GOD AND OURSELVES: The account of Isaiah's vision is significant for Christians today in two main ways. First, it offers the most illuminating

[1] *The Book of Isaiah* (New York: Harper & Bros. n. d.) , I, 80. Used by permission.

interpretation in all literature of *the meaning of worship at its best*. Whether alone or in a group, the true worshiper lives through experiences remarkably like those of the prophet. To stand in the presence of the holy God, adoring him for his own sake, is to become painfully aware of our own unworthiness. This consciousness wrings from our hearts a humble confession of sin, which opens the way for the experience of cleansing and forgiveness. Our broken relation to God restored, we offer our lives to him in grateful dedication: "Here am I; send me!" Then follows the divine imperative, "*Go!*" The specific *action* to which we are summoned may be less clear and less dramatic than it was for Isaiah, though fully as difficult. But as we seek to understand and perform it, the God we find in worship will give the needed strength. It is revealing to note how closely the stages in Isaiah's call are paralleled in the elements found in our Sunday morning services of worship. How genuinely do they describe what happens within us? Is our worship actually a living, personal encounter with God?

More broadly, Isaiah's call raises forcibly—and answers—*the question of our own call*. There is deep suggestiveness in the fact that the seraph touched and cleansed the prophet's lips not with a glowing ember, but with a hearthstone of the type used by Hebrew women in baking. The divine presence makes all things sacred. God can touch life in homes no less than in temples, and hearth as well as altar may be a holy place. The divine summons is not limited to prophets or ecstatic visions. Rather, we are all called to enter into fellowship with God and to serve him in every phase of our common life.

The young minister seeking full membership in a Methodist Annual Conference is asked, "Are you resolved to devote yourself wholly to God and his work?" Should not every Christian be able to answer "Yes" to this question? The fact that we assign special functions to ordained clergymen has unfortunately led us to assume that they alone are ministers. Actually, there is an equally important ministry of the laity, a "priesthood of all believers" in which we are called to minister not primarily to ourselves, but to each other in God's name. This ministry is rendered in the ordinary associations of men and women, in home, field, shop, factory, office, school, hospital—wherever the people of God[1] in word and deed witness to their faith and manifest the love of God in love to men. "Full-time Christian service" is the privilege and responsibility of all the followers of Christ. To it are called not only those who serve in church-related occupations but equally those—more than 99 percent of the Church—whose God-given talents fit them best for other forms of worthy work. To all of us the holy God says, "*Go!*"

THE LIFE

It is possible to distinguish three main periods in the prophetic ministry of Isaiah:

[1] This is a frequent *New Testament* definition of the church. From *laos*, the Greek word for people, we derive our word laity.

28

1. His early ministry, from his call to the beginning of the reign of Ahaz, 742-735 B.C.

2. Prophetic activity relating to the Syro-Ephraimite war and its results, from the attack of Judah until the fall of Samaria and the end of the kingdom of Israel, 735-721 B.C.

3. Prophecies occasioned by the rebellions against Assyria and the resultant invasions of Palestine, 721-701 B.C. (or 690 B.C.).

The next three chapters will deal respectively with these three periods in the life of Isaiah. An additional chapter will consider the "messianic" prophecies of Isaiah 1 through 39, which are difficult to assign with any assurance to specific periods; it will also summarize the chief religious teachings of Isaiah. At the beginning of each chapter will be listed biblical passages which are relevant to the period.

III

THE LORD EXALTED
IN JUSTICE

Isaiah 1:21-31; 2:6 through 4:11;
5:1-24a; 6:1-13; 10:17-23

As THE reign of Jotham began, both Judah and
Israel were enjoying great material prosperity,
attended, however, by glaring social evils. The recent absence of Assyrian armies from the west had
produced a false sense of security and an unrealis-
tic optimism which dulled ethical sensitivity. In
such a situation it was natural that the prophet
with a commission from the Lord of righteousness
should begin his ministry by denouncing injustice.
The early message of Isaiah broadly resembled that
of Amos, his older contemporary in the northern
kingdom. He attacked the social sins of his country and warned of their inevitable consequence in
national disaster.

However, in one respect Isaiah's early preaching
reached a deeper level than that of Amos. He regarded covetousness, love of luxury, and indifference to the plight of the poor as symptoms of a

more *fundamental evil—disloyalty to the Lord*. Such evils sprang from a refusal to recognize the divine rule—the substitution of faith in man's own devices and resources for trust in God. Greed, for example, is evil not only because it causes human suffering, or even because it violates the will of a God whose holiness is essentially ethical, but still more because it is a rejection of God by men who prefer their own ways to his.

GOD'S JUDGMENT ON JUDAH

INJUSTICE AND DEGENERATE LIVING: Isaiah pronounces judgment on Judah for a variety of sins. The evils are specifically listed, though punishment is announced in general terms, ordinarily metaphorical. Jerusalem, intended by God to be "the faithful city" which serves him in justice, "has become a harlot" (1:21-31). Her leaders do not hesitate to murder or steal to accomplish their selfish ends. Bribes and special privileges are accepted and even sought, while orphans and widows have no one to defend them. Those who thus forsake the Lord shall be consumed; they shall wither "like a garden without water." "The strong shall become tow"—coarse flax ready for spinning, which burns readily.

Elders and princes, "the mighty man and the soldier, the judge and the prophet, the diviner and the elder," captains, counselors, men of rank, and magicians—all are guilty of exploiting the people and "grinding the face of the poor" (3:1-15). Rulers guilty of such deeds have offended God himself; they will inevitably stumble and fall. The result will be anarchy and a leaderless people: "I will make boys their princes, and babes shall rule over them." This suggests the chaos which in the ancient world always ensued when the leaders of a nation were carried into captivity by a victorious invader, but the prophet does not definitely predict this.

Isaiah is incensed also by the conduct of the economically privileged women of Jerusalem (3:16 through 4:1). Smug and arrogant, they walk the streets "mincing along as they go," casting flirtatious glances, and attracting attention by bells on their ankles. The list of ornamental jewelry and the fashionable garments in their extravagant wardrobes would do credit to the stocks of those shops which cater to the vanity of today's elite. But all this finery, so beloved by the irresponsible wealthy, the Lord will take away:

> Instead of perfume there will be rottenness;
> and instead of a girdle, a rope;
> and instead of well-set hair, baldness;
> and instead of a rich robe, a girding of sack-
> cloth;
> instead of beauty, shame.

The male population will be so decimated in battle that seven women will compete for the favors of one man, asking nothing but to be called his wife. Love of luxury and primary devotion to physical beauty are in the end self-defeating.

Isaiah sternly condemns those who multiply houses and lands in flagrant disregard of the needs of other people and the welfare of the community (5:8-10):

> Woe to those who join house to house,
>   who add field to field,
> until there is no more room.

They cannot escape the judgment of "the Lord of hosts" who "is exalted in justice," or the moral law of the God who "shows himself holy in righteousness" (5:16). The practicer of economic injustice flouts the Lord of history. Ultimately he accomplishes his own undoing.

In *Les Misérables* Victor Hugo writes that it was impossible for Napoleon to win the battle of Waterloo. "Why? Because of Wellington? Because of Bluecher? No! Because of God." The "excessive weight" of this arrogant conqueror had "disturbed the equilibrium" of the moral order. "Napoleon had been impeached before the infinite and his fall was decreed. He vexed God."[1]

According to Isaiah, covetousness vexes God. Therefore the wealthy who seek isolation on big estates get more isolation than they bargain for, with no workers near to produce the necessities of life.

> Surely many houses shall be desolate,
>   large and beautiful houses, without
>   inhabitant.

Furthermore, the lands which are short-sightedly overworked for quick gain rapidly become exhausted and barren. Ten acres of vineyard will yield only one bath—a mere six gallons—of wine, while a homer of seed will yield only an ephah. Since a homer is about ten bushels and an ephah one bushel, this means that nine-tenths of the seed

[1] *Les Misérables* (New York: A. L. Burt Co., n. d.), I, 337-38.

sown will be wasted. So thorough will be the deterioration that roots as well as fruits will die (5:24):

> Therefore, as the tongue of fire devours the stubble,
>   and as dry grass sinks down in the flame,
> so their root will be as rottenness,
>   and their blossom go up like dust.

Isaiah's words are the voice of the Lord for our time as for his. Twice in a generation we have created dust bowls through excessive deforestation and the failure to practice crop rotation and other conservation procedures. "The earth is the Lord's and the fulness thereof" (Psa. 24:1); it will not cooperate when men try to exploit it for quick profit, forgetting the welfare of later generations. In recent years large corporation farms have steadily displaced farm families who owned and cultivated their own lands, transforming them into agricultural tenants or industrial workers, with profound danger to the stability of rural life.

The prophet denounces also those who flout justice where it should be most upheld—the courts of law. The guilty may buy their liberty from corrupt judges, while the innocent are deprived of their rights, and helpless orphans and widows have no protection. Hence those who fail to judge righteously will themselves be judged righteously, and it will be for them a time of woe (5:23; 1:23).

Isaiah's criticisms are not limited to the wealthy and the powerful. Among the offenders not only are "their honored men . . . dying of hunger," but "their multitude is parched with thirst"; the "throngs" of Jerusalem no less than her nobility

34

face punishment (5:13-14). It is "man" who is bowed down, and "men" who are brought low (2:9). Included, for example, are the carousers

who rise early in the morning,
    that they may run after strong drink,
who tarry late into the evening
    till wine inflames them!

Such persons are "heroes at drinking wine," but they lack the courage to live soberly, because "they do not regard the deeds of the LORD" (5:11-12).

Another form of degeneration that cuts across the whole population is the blurring of moral distinctions through persistence in wrongdoing:

Woe to those who call evil good
    and good evil,
who put darkness for light
    and light for darkness,
who put bitter for sweet
    and sweet for bitter! (5:20)

Here is the prophetic equivalent of the sin against the Holy Spirit which cannot be forgiven (Matt. 12:31-32; Mark 3:29; Luke 12:10). He who stifles the voice of God and continues in evil may reach the point where to him evil is good. Such sin is unpardonable, not because God lacks mercy, but because the sinner, no longer capable of seeing his need for forgiveness, cannot experience the repentance which is the condition of forgiveness.

DISLOYALTY TO GOD: For Isaiah the evils we have listed are not strung loosely together like beads on a necklace; they are plants which spring from the common soil of religious apostasy. All are forms of the *one basic sin of disloyalty to God* (Isa. 1:2-4). This faithlessness appears in part in the idol-worship which was widespread in eighth-century Judah. The fertility deities and the cult of sacred oaks and groves still claimed their devotees. The prophet laments that the land of the Lord's people is full of idols:

> They bow down to the work of their hands,
> to what their own fingers have made (2:8).

Isaiah truly discerns, however, that such practices themselves reflect a deeper distortion. Idol worship is at bottom a form of self-worship. The prophet's sharpest invective is directed against the arrogant *man-centeredness* of those who put themselves in the place of God, "defying his glorious presence" (3:8). So stubbornly attached are they to their sins that they "drag their guilt after them, like a bullock on a rope, and their sin, like a heifer on a lead."[1] Meanwhile, affecting the language of piety, they conceitedly call on the Lord, whose effectiveness and very existence they question, to make his purpose known:

> "Let him speed his work
> that we may see it;
> let the purpose of the Holy One of Israel
> draw near,
> and let it come, that we may know it!"
> (5:19)

But such insolent boastfulness cannot endure. However shrewd men may be in their own eyes (5:21), they are not self-sufficient.

> For the LORD of hosts has a day
> against all that is proud and lofty,

· · · · · · · · · · · ·

[1] This is R. B. Y. Scott's suggestive translation of 5:18, in *The Interpreter's Bible*, V, 202.

And the haughtiness of man shall be humbled,
and the pride of men shall be
brought low;
and the LORD alone will be exalted in that
day.
And the idols shall utterly pass away.
And men shall enter the caves of the rocks
and the holes of the ground,
from before the terror of the LORD (2:12, 17-19).

Here again the prophet is speaking to our day as well as his. Wise in our own sight and proud of our own ability, we have learned the secret of atomic power, but do little to relate its application to the will of him who is the source of all power. Like Prometheus, we have stolen fire from heaven, but unlike the hero of the Greek myth we are more intent on developing its destructive possibilities than on using it for human good.

For us, too, the Lord has a day—which we ourselves may bring by persisting in our wilful pride and trusting in our own might. For a time we talked of building underground shelters, but already we know that "the caves of the rocks" offer no defense against radioactive dust. There is no place to hide, yet we blindly persist in building bigger bombs, in the vain hope of scaring off our potential enemy, who does the same. If we refuse to turn from our foolish ways, the desolation of which Isaiah speaks will afflict not Palestine only, but the whole earth, and not for a generation or two, but for centuries to come. This is not idle chatter, but imminent possibility. This will be indeed "the terror of the LORD"—not the angry retaliation of a vindictive

God, but the sorrowful discipline of a loving but righteous Father, who allows his rebellious children to suffer the consequences of their own sinful choice.

Isaiah attacks, in addition to idolatry, even the approved worship of the temple if it is unaccompanied by right living (1:10-17). The most elaborate ritualistic acts are worse than vain when allowed to become a substitute for justice. "Trampling" of the Lord's courts—ceremony for its own sake—is an abomination to God. He will not see the sacrifices nor hear the prayers of those whose "hands are full of blood." Hence the eloquent exhortation:

> Wash yourselves, make yourselves clean;
>> remove the evil of your doings
>> from before my eyes;
> cease to do evil,
>> learn to do good;
> seek justice,
>> correct oppression;
> defend the fatherless,
>> plead for the widow.

WILD GRAPES IN THE LORD'S VINEYARD: A fitting epitome of Isaiah's condemnation of injustice is his song of the vineyard (5:1-7; see Matt. 21:33-46 and parallels). The passage pictures the loving intention of God for his people, Judah's proud rejection of the divine will, the destruction to which her unrighteousness leads, and the sadness and pathos with which the Lord abandons his venture.

In language perhaps borrowed in irony from the fertility cults which threatened Israel's worship of one good God, Isaiah sings for his "beloved" a "love song concerning his vineyard." He portrays the care with which the owner cleared a fertile hill, planted it with selected vines, built a tower to guard it, and hewed a vat to receive the wine. But when the harvest came the vines yielded wild grapes. "What more was there to do for my vineyard?" asks the Lord.

> When I looked for it to yield grapes
> why did it yield wild grapes?

However, in the deep pain of his disappointment God is not sentimental. He acts to destroy the vineyard, removing its hedge and wall so that it is trampled down, ceasing to cultivate it so that briers crowd out the vines, and cutting off the rains without which it cannot grow. For the Lord's vineyard, "his pleasant planting," is Judah,

> and he looked for justice (*mishpat*),
>   but behold, bloodshed (*mispah*);
> for righteousness (*cedhagah*),
>   but behold, a cry (*ceagah*).

The two word-pairs constitute a double play on words which cannot be adequately rendered in English. G. H. Box approximates it with his translation:

> For measures He looked—but lo massacres!
> For right—but lo riot![1]

Holy love cannot tolerate such rebelliousness.

Thus the central message of the parable, like that of all Isaiah's early preaching, is one of divine judgment on human unrighteousness, seen as a rejection of God's purpose for man.

[1] *The Book of Isaiah* (New York: The Macmillan Co., 1909), p. 41. Used by permission of the publisher.

However, hope is not totally absent. Because the Hebrew of 1:18 is obscure, there is no agreement concerning the meaning of these familiar words. Yet it is hard to avoid treating them as a genuine offer of pardon. Perhaps 1:18-20 can be truly paraphrased as follows: "Let's talk this over. Do you mean to say that though your sins are scarlet they shall become white—without any change in your attitude? If so, you are mocking God. His mercy is not automatic, and it does not ignore the demands of righteousness. He is always ready to forgive, but cannot unless your repentance prepares you to receive his forgiveness. If you turn from your sin and show your penitence by obedience to God, your crimson sin will become pure like wool. But if you flout God's will, you are lost."

In this spirit of realistic promise, the prophet looks for a day when Zion, again a "faithful city,"

> shall be redeemed by justice,
>> and those in her who repent, by
>> righteousness (1:26-27).

It is also significant that during this period he named his first child Shear-jashub (a remnant will return). Yet when he introduces the idea of the remnant it is probably more as a threat than as a promise: "*only* a remnant of them will return." Though eventually a few will turn to the Lord, now "destruction is decreed," fulfilling the divine righteousness. "For the Lord . . . will make a full end . . . in the midst of all the earth" (10:20-23).

IV

SWIFT BOOTY, SPEEDY PREY

Isaiah 5:24b-30; 7 and 8; 9:8 through 10:4;
17:1-6, 9-11; 28:1-4;
II Kings 15:17 through 17:6;
II Chronicles 28:1-4, 16-27.

I N 735 B. C. kings Rezin of Syria and Pekah of
Israel sought the support of Judah in a coalition
against Assyria. When Ahaz, either neutral or pro-
Assyrian, refused to take part, the two kingdoms
to the north moved to attack Judah, apparently
hoping to bring Ahaz to terms or to replace him
with a puppet who would join their alliance. Ahaz
and the citizens of Judah were terror-stricken. In
this critical situation Isaiah's prophetic ministry
entered a new phase. He adopted the role of political counselor, seeking to guide the king in a course
harmonious with the will of God.

Ahaz proposed to secure the help of Assyrian
might, and thus to remove the threat by confront-
ing his enemies with a larger threat. This natural
but short-sighted policy aroused the vigorous opposition of Isaiah, who exposed its weakness and

41

offered his own positive alternatives. Three of his utterances were accompanied by symbolic actions or "signs."

ISAIAH AND THE
SYRO-EPHRAMITE WAR

A CALL TO TRUST IN GOD: Before Isaiah's time an aqueduct had been built to carry water from the spring Gihon, in the Kidron Valley below the eastern wall of Jerusalem, to a reservoir on the southern edge of the city. Like any leader of a people threatened with siege, Ahaz was concerned about his water supply. One day, as he was inspecting the lower end of the conduit, he was suddenly confronted by Isaiah, who under a sense of divine command had brought with him his little son, Shear-jashub. The boy had been given his symbolic name at birth, probably to dramatize his father's conviction that only a few would prove faithful to the Lord. Now he again became a living oracle, reminding Ahaz of the dark future to which his policy, if persisted in, would lead: only a remnant would survive.

Isaiah's spoken word to Ahaz is an admonition to trust in God: "Take heed, be quiet, do not fear, and do not let your heart be faint" (7:4). The attacking kings are no more than "smoldering stumps of fire-brands," almost burned out and therefore not really dangerous. Even at their best their power is but human, and they are no match for the God who is ultimately the Ruler of human history. *The way of true security* is not trust in superior military might, but *faith in God and a national life based on his righteous will*. If Judah trusts Assyria instead, she is lost:

'If you will not believe,
surely you shall not be established' (7:1-9).

The oracle is a play on words. The root *aman* with one stem means to trust or believe, while with another stem, only slightly different in sound, it means to be confirmed or established. G. H. Box reproduces the Hebrew form suggestively: "Verily if thou have no strong trust—no trusty stronghold shall be thine!"[1] Elmer A. Leslie translates it: "If you will not confide, surely you cannot abide."[2] John Edgar McFadyen renders it simply: "No faith, no fixity."[3]

THE SIGN OF IMMANUEL: On another occasion Isaiah invited Ahaz to ask for confirmation of his message in a "sign" or token from the Lord (7:10-17). Pretending piety, the king replied that he would not test the Lord. Fully aware of Ahaz's actual unbelief and disobedience, Isaiah declared that God himself would send a sign: a young woman will conceive and bear a son, and will name him Immanuel (God is with us). However, before the child is old enough to distinguish good from evil,[4] the lands whose kings Ahaz now dreads will be desolate. Judah too will be overrun and laid

[1] *The Book of Isaiah*, p. 47.
[2] *The Prophets Tell Their Own Story* (New York: The Abingdon Press, 1939), p. 93. Used by permission.
[3] *The Book of the Prophecies of Isaiah*, (The Bible for Home and School. New York: The Macmillan Co., 1910), p. 72. Used by permission of the publisher.
[4] Some commentators believe that the reference is not to ethical distinctions, but to the ability of the child, after weaning at the age of two or three, to choose the foods which suit his taste.

43

waste. Since ordinary agriculture will then be impossible, the child will have to subsist on curds and honey, the primitive food of refugees in the wilderness. The sign is thus at once an assurance of the presence and power of God, in whom Ahaz is called to trust, and a warning of the privations which will ensue if such trust is lacking.

Traditionally many Christians have found in this passage a prediction of the coming of Jesus as the Messiah, and of the virgin birth. Support for this view has been found in Matthew 1:23, one of several instances where the evangelist quotes a prophetic passage, without particular attention to its original context, to show that the life of Jesus Christ fulfills Old Testament expectations (see Hos. 11:1; Matt. 2:15). However, Matthew's quotation is based not on the Hebrew text of Isaiah 7:14, but on the Septuagint version which inaccurately uses the Greek word *parthenos*, virgin, to translate the Hebrew, *almah*. This Hebrew term means simply a maiden, a young woman of marriageable age, possibly, but by no means necessarily, a virgin. Had Isaiah wanted to specify unmistakably a miraculous birth from a virgin, he would have had to use the Hebrew *bethulah*; instead he uses *almah*, which is correctly translated in our Revised Standard Version as "young woman."

Two other considerations indicate that it would be a misrepresentation to regard 7:10-17 as a specific foretelling of the birth of Jesus. For one thing, the child is named Immanuel as a *sign* or *token* of the deliverance of Judah, but he is not himself the deliverer, whereas Jesus Christ is. Secondly, a

44

prediction by Isaiah of the appearance of the Messiah more than several hundred years later could not have been a sign to Ahaz in 735 B.C. Isaiah's oracles, like those of the other great prophets, were addressed to specific historical situations and designed to meet the needs of his contemporaries. The forecast of an event in the remote future could have meant little to those whose faith he sought to arouse.

This leaves the way completely open for us, like the gospel writers, to see in Jesus Christ the true and ultimate fulfillment of the Jewish messianic hope, and likewise to apply to him imagery which originally had other connotations. The name Immanuel, for example, is justly precious to Christian believers. Hardly any other word sums up so perfectly the significance of him through whom, as the Word made flesh, God acted in human life and history to reconcile the world to himself.

Indeed, we may have in this incident the dawn in Isaiah's consciousness of the messianic expectation which he develops so eloquently in several other passages (2:2-4; 9:1-7; 11:1-9; 32:1-8, 15-20). The identity of the young woman referred to remains a mystery. The reference may be quite general, meaning that young women will bear children and name them "Immanuel"; or it may be to some specific person known to Ahaz—Isaiah's wife, a member of the royal house, or a new wife of Ahaz himself. (Several ancient versions read "*thou* shalt call his name.") In any event, the central truth of the "sign" is that the early birth, name, and experience of Immanuel will confirm the truth of Isaiah's message. The fact that the expectation was not realized when and as the prophet expected is no serious problem. The course of events did validate his assertion of the presence of God in those events. Samaria and Damascus were speedily overthrown, the policy followed by Judah did prove disastrous, and the dream of a messianic king was ultimately fulfilled in a manner far more glorious than Isaiah himself could envision.

A MESSAGE OF DOOM: A third symbolic action predicted the imminent destruction of Damascus and Samaria, specifying the Assyrian king as the agent (8:1-4). Isaiah felt led by God to write plainly on a large tablet or board the words *Maher-shalal-hashbaz*. The first two parts of the inscription are Hebrew and the last two Aramaic, but with the same meaning: Swift-spoil-quick-prey, or Hasty the spoiling, speedy the plundering. This act he had witnessed by two reliable persons. Later, when his second son was born, he was directed to use the same words in naming the child. Before the infant had learned to speak the names of his parents, the wealth of Israel and Syria would be carried away as spoil.

In the vivid passage immediately following, Isaiah applies this message of doom to Judah, finding effective symbolism in the contrast between the quiet flow of the waters of Shiloah (through the rock-hewn conduit from the spring Gihon to the pool below) and the turbulent waters of the mighty Euphrates (8:5-8a). The nation refuses to trust the invisible working of God, preferring to rely rather on the violent power of Assyria. Therefore the Assyrian flood waters will overflow their banks and engulf even distant Judah.

In several other brief oracles Isaiah predicts the destruction to come "in that day" (7:18-25; see 17:1-6, 9-11). The invaders are likened to swarms of flies and hornets which will come from Egypt and Assyria to ravage the land. The disciplinary work of God in coming events is seen in the action of the Assyrian king—a razor hired by the Lord to do a thorough job in shaving Israel. The result will be ruin: formerly fertile fields overgrown with briers and thorns; and a decimated population barely existing on wild honey, the milk produced by a few lean cattle, and the small animals the hunter can kill.

AHAZ'S DISASTROUS ALLIANCE: Isaiah's counsel fell on deaf ears. Desperate with terror, Ahaz sent to Tiglath-pileser, the Assyrian ruler, messengers who vowed homage to him and pleaded with him to rescue Judah. The plea was accompanied by gifts of gold and silver from the temple and the king's palace (II Kings 16:7-9; II Chron. 28:21). Ahaz also sought supernatural help, restoring the Baal-Astarte cults of early Canaan and introducing other idolatrous rites. He even reverted to the ancient heathen practice of human sacrifice and "burned his son as an offering" (II Kings 16:3; II Chron. 28:3). Here is dramatic though pathetic proof of Ahaz's spiritual bankruptcy. Refusing to trust in the God whose presence was symbolized in the birth of one child, Immanuel, he sought pagan aid through the death of another son.

Judah's rescue was dearly bought. True, in 734 B.C. Assyrian forces invaded northern Israel, annexed the territory east of the Jordan, and reduced the land to an area approximately thirty by forty miles. Many of the inhabitants were deported and replaced with people brought from other lands. In 732 B.C. Damascus was captured and Syria was crushed. However, the result for Judah was not freedom, but vassalage to Assyria, the annual payment of tribute, constant danger of occupation, and exposure to the insidious influence of Assyrian religion.

Ahaz soon installed in the temple at Jerusalem a copy of an Assyrian altar which impressed him at Damascus. In deference to the Assyrians, he also made other changes in the temple furniture and forms of worship. Although the overwhelming disaster envisaged by Isaiah did not occur as soon as he expected, Judah was now ignominiously subject to Assyria, and within a generation the course chosen by Ahaz culminated in the calamitous invasion of Sennacherib. The chronicler's report is simple but eloquent: Tiglath-pileser "came against him, and afflicted him instead of strengthening him" (II Chron. 28:20).

Thus developments abundantly confirmed the soundness of Isaiah's advice. The folly of Ahaz's program was all the greater because his turn to Assyria was quite unnecessary. Judah incurred thereby an obligation to Tiglath-pileser for military action which the Assyrian monarch would almost certainly have taken anyway to end a coalition which was actually directed at him. Self-interest alone would have forced him to suppress subject nations who were attempting a war of conquest on their own account. Had Ahaz shared Isaiah's faith, the nation would have been delivered without humiliation. Hence the prophet's counsel, grounded in trust in God, was really the maturest political wisdom.

Confronted by the complete rejection of his program, the prophet was given an insight of deep import for later religion. He felt called to proclaim: "Do not call conspiracy all that this people call conspiracy, and do not fear what they fear, nor be in dread. But the LORD of hosts, him you shall regard as holy; let him be your fear, and let him be your dread. And he will become a sanctuary, and a stone of offence, and a rock of stumbling to both houses of Israel" (Isa. 8:11-14). Because of linguistic problems the precise meaning of this passage is not certain. However, Isaiah seems to be summoning faithful men—an inner group of his followers or a larger company—to reject the fear-inspired policy of the majority and to make instead an alliance with God. An accurate paraphrase might read: "Do not dread the conspiracy of the Syrians and Ephraimites, and in panic attempt to thwart it by conspiring with Assyria. Conspire rather with the Lord, and fear him alone. Those who do, will find in him their true security, but those who refuse will meet disaster."

Isaiah is here a precursor of Peter, who almost eight centuries later was to declare: "We must

49

obey God rather than men" (Acts 5:29). R. B. Y. Scott writes: "This is apparently the first summons to men in the history of biblical religion to separate themselves in spirit from their social group in obedience to God. It was a moment pregnant with significance for the future histories of Judaism and of the Christian church."[1]

Isaiah apparently followed his appeal with appropriate action. Realizing the uselessness of further public teaching for the time being, he turned his energies in two other directions. He completed the record of his prophetic utterances up to this time, and formed a small inner circle of followers who would embody in life the message he had proclaimed in words. In graphic language he tells of his decision: "Bind up the testimony, seal the teaching among my disciples. I will wait for the LORD, who is hiding his face from the house of Jacob, and I will hope in him. Behold, I and the children whom the LORD has given me are signs and portents in Israel from the LORD of hosts, who dwells on Mount Zion" (Isa. 8:16-18).

When a scroll was not to be used for a time but preserved for future use, it was customarily tied with a cord or sealed, just as we deposit deeds and other valuable documents in envelopes or boxes for later reference. Having committed his prophecies to writing, Isaiah would wait patiently for history to demonstrate their truth. Meanwhile, that truth would be preserved and deepened in living documents—in Isaiah and his sons whose very names spoke eloquently, and in a little band

[1] Exegesis of Isaiah 1-39, *The Interpreter's Bible*, V, 226.

of loyal disciples or apprentices.[1] The faithful remnant of which he had spoken thus became real, at least in embryo, in his own lifetime.

The formation of this spiritual fellowship during Isaiah's temporary retirement from public life may have been the most influential act of his whole career. With it emerged for the first time a religious community which was no longer simply the political community functioning religiously, but something quite distinct. The group practice of religion was freed from its connection with civic life. Out of this simple beginning was to grow eventually the separation of church and state.

More immediately, the little company was a partial realization in the prophet's own lifetime of the faithful "remnant" for which he had hoped. It might be called the first cell group in history. Growing and reproducing, it nurtured through successive national crises that living faith which became Israel's greatest legacy to mankind. Rufus Jones believed that Jeremiah a century later was a product of this movement.[2] Possibly the unknown prophet of the exile was also a member of this redemptive fellowship, and thus a true spiritual descendant of its founder. If so, he is with singular appropriateness called the Second Isaiah.

THE DOWNFALL OF ISRAEL

How long Isaiah refrained from public activity we do not know. However, it could hardly have

[1] Martin Buber's translation of the Hebrew *limmudim*, which is used as a noun nowhere else in the Old Testament except here and in 50 4. See *The Prophetic Faith*, p. 204.

[2] Rufus Jones, *A Call to What is Vital* (New York: The Macmillan Co., 1949), p. 58.

been much more than ten years, since some of his oracles of judgment on Ephraim mean most if they are assigned to the period just before the fall of Samaria in 722-721 B.C. About 732 B.C., after an internal uprising in which Pekah was assassinated, Tiglath-pileser placed Hoshea on the throne of Israel. When in 727 B.C. Shalmaneser IV succeeded to the Assyrian throne, Hoshea joined Egypt in a revolt against him which was swiftly quelled. Chafing under the yoke and forced to pay new tribute, Israel rebelled again within two years. This time Hoshea was promptly imprisoned and Samaria was besieged. The capital held out during three years of privation, but finally fell to Sargon II, who had become king of Assyria on the death of Shalmaneser in 722 B.C. This meant also the end of the kingdom of Israel, which became an Assyrian province. Twenty-seven thousand of its citizens were deported and replaced by people from other parts of the empire (II Kings 17:1-6). The result was eventually the growth of a hybrid population—the Samaritans with whom the "pure" Jews of Jesus' day would "have no dealings."

Living only about thirty-five miles from Samaria, Isaiah was inevitably stirred by these shattering events. Both Israel and Judah were Hebrew nations, in spite of their divided existence since Solomon's reign. Isaiah sensed also that the bell he heard tolling so somberly for Israel tolled for Judah as well. There is deep sorrow in the stern judgments which he pronounces on "the fading flower" of the "glorious beauty" of his northern neighbor (Isa. 28:1).

From this period probably come the solemn oracles of 9:8 through 10:4 and 5:24b-30, the latter probably the incomplete original conclusion of the former. Three stanzas narrate past events which exemplify the sins and punishments of Israel. The next two shift attention to Judah, warning that her doom impends also if her citizens do not mend their ways. In words reminiscent of his early denunciations of unrighteousness, Isaiah pronounces woe to those who oppress the needy and deny justice to widows and orphans. They face inevitable judgment, which will come in the form of earthquake or pestilence as well as invasion. Each stanza in this crescendo of disaster concludes with the dark refrain:

> For all this his anger is not turned away
> and his hand is stretched out still.

Then follows one of the most graphic pieces of poetic description in the entire Old Testament (5:26-30). Having persisted in rejecting God, Judah must now reap the fruit of her sin. The Lord's instrument of judgment is the superbly trained and conditioned Assyrian army:

> And lo, swiftly, speedily it comes!
> None is weary, none stumbles,
>   none slumbers or sleeps,
> not a waistcloth is loose,
>   not a sandal-thong broken;
> their arrows are sharp,
>   all their bows bent,
> their horses' hoofs seem like flint,
>   and their wheels like the whirlwind.

Like lions they seize their prey, and rescue is impossible. The whole land is engulfed in darkness and distress.

V

IN TRUST SHALL BE
YOUR STRENGTH

Isaiah 1:7-9; 10:5-16, 24-34; 14:24-32;
17:12-14; 18:1-6; 20:1-6; 22:1-25;
28:7-29; 29:1-16; 30:1-17, 27-33;
31:1-5, 8-9; 32:9-14; 36 through 39;
II Kings 18:13 through 20:21.

O NCE Judah had lost her independence, Isaiah
believed that the same divine judgment that had
brought her under Assyrian rule required her to
endure it. He therefore emphatically opposed her
attempted revolts. Such attempts set the stage for
the third major phase of his prophetic ministry.

RUMBLINGS OF REVOLT

In 713 B.C. the cities of Philistia, led by Ashdod,
sought the co-operation of Judah in a rebellion
against Sargon instigated by Egypt and Ethiopia.
For three years Isaiah went naked and barefoot, or
wearing at most the loincloth and light shirt of a
slave, to dramatize his warning that the Jews as

well as their allies would become captives and slaves if they joined the revolt (20:2-4). He was convinced that though God's purpose required the eventual overthrow of Assyria, the time had not yet come. A signal would one day be given; in the meantime, the path of wisdom was not recourse to human alliances, but quiet trust in God, whose purposes would slowly ripen like fruit in summer (18:1-6).

One of the leaders of the pro-Ethiopian party in Judah was Shebna, the king's treasurer. He was apparently so impressed by Egyptian power and pomp and so eager to share in it that, like the Pharaohs, he hewed out of rock a tomb for himself. Repelled by this grandiose act, Isaiah denounced Shebna and declared that the Lord would remove him from office and name Eliakim treasurer (22:15-25). This change actually occurred (36:22; II Kings 18:18), and it may have been followed by a temporary decline in Egyptian influence at the king's court. This could account for the fact that, when Sargon in 711 B.C. struck in the west, captured Ashdod, deported its inhabitants, and dispelled the uprising, Judah was unharmed.

Several years later Hezekiah became so critically ill that his death seemed inevitable. Faced by this prospect, he wept and prayed fervently, citing his faithfulness to the Lord. Isaiah now received an assurance that the king would live, and so informed him. At the prophet's suggestion a fig poultice was applied to the inflamed boil, and Hezekiah recovered (38:1-5, 21; II Kings 20:1-11).

In the meantime the Chaldean Merodach-bala-dan, previously deposed as king of Babylon, had regained his throne. In 705 B.C. he sought to stir up a general revolt against Sennacherib, who had just succeeded Sargon as king of Assyria. Ostensibly to congratulate Hezekiah on his recovery, he sent envoys to Jerusalem with letters and gifts. Deceived by this flattery, the king foolishly showed them all the national resources. Isaiah, however, correctly perceived the embassy's hidden purpose, and warned Hezekiah that such folly would result in the removal to Babylon of the country's wealth and the king's own sons. Callously indifferent to the welfare of the coming generation, the king interpreted this as a good prediction. "For he thought, 'Why not, if there will be peace and security in my days?'" (39:1-8; II Kings 20:12-20; II Chron. 32:31). Though desperate when he faced the prospect of his own death, and eager for personal security, he cared little if his policies brought suffering to his descendants. The incident reveals vividly the problem faced by Isaiah as he sought to counsel this ruler, who saw only the hours, from the perspective of the long years of God.

EGYPT OR GOD?

The spirit of revolt spread steadily, and Judah's political leaders were in full sympathy. For support they looked chiefly to Egypt, who welcomed such overtures, since she herself would gladly have displaced Assyria as the great world power. Some of Isaiah's most eloquent oracles were called forth

by the efforts of the Judean officials, at first in
secret, to conclude an alliance with Egypt against
Assyria. With all his energy he opposed this plan,
for two main reasons.

In the first place, though outwardly it was rebellion against Assyria, more truly it was rebellion
against God. It was an effort to evade the divine
discipline and to wrest from the Lord of history his
control over the destinies of men:

"Woe to the rebellious children," says the Lord,
"who carry out a plan, but not mine;
and who make a league, but not of my spirit,
that they may add sin to sin;
who set out to go down to Egypt,
without asking for my counsel" (30:1-2).

Preferring their own plans to "the instruction of
the Lord," and resenting the counsel of Isaiah, the
rebellious people called on their seers to see no
more and on their prophets to stop prophesying:

"Leave the way, turn aside from the path,
let us hear no more of the Holy One of Israel."
(30:9-11).

Yet, in rejecting the Holy One of Israel, the
Judean nobility were flouting his moral order and
paving the way to their own ruin. They were making "a covenant with death" (28:15). Therefore
Isaiah opposed their policy secondarily because he
knew it would be self-defeating. He agreed with
the earlier judgment of Sargon, that the king of
Egypt was "a potentate, incapable to save them";[1]
and with the later declaration of Sennacherib's

[1] James B. Pritchard (ed.), *Ancient Near Eastern Texts Relating to the
Old Testament* (Princeton: Princeton University Press, 1950), p. 287.
Used by permission.

57

chief of staff, that Egypt was "a broken reed of a staff, which will pierce the hand of any man who leans on it" (36:6). In God alone lay Judah's real security. The true Zion could be built only on faith. In its foundation was a cornerstone inscribed, "He who believes will not be in haste"; and its walls would be kept true by the plummet line of righteousness (28:16-17). The sound course for Judah lay in submission to Assyrian rule as a divine discipline, repentant correction of the wrongs which produced it, trustful obedience to God's will, and quiet waiting for the time when God himself would act to deliver her:

> In returning and rest you shall be saved;
> in quietness and trust shall be your strength
> (30:15).

Rejecting Isaiah's program as hopelessly impractical, the politicians blindly placed their trust in military alliances, honoring the Lord with their lips while their hearts were far from him (29:9-10,13). The prophet saw clearly the weakness as well as the godlessness of this "realistic" policy. Its collapse would be like that of a piece of pottery, smashed so badly that no fragment remains large enough "to take fire from the hearth" or "dip up water out of the cistern" (30:13-14). It would ruin Judah and Egypt alike.

> Woe to those who go down to Egypt for help
> and rely on horses,
> who trust in chariots because they are many
> and in horsemen because they are very strong,
> but do not look to the Holy One of Israel
> or consult the LORD! (31:1).

They fail to reckon with the God whose righteous power overthrows the evildoer, and against whom no merely human wisdom can avail.

> The Egyptians are men, and not God;
>> and their horses are flesh, and not spirit.
> When the Lord stretches out his hand,
>> the helper will stumble, and he who is helped
>> will fall,
> and they will all perish together (31:2-3).

Can discerning Christians fail to perceive the disturbing parallel between the policies relied on in Isaiah's day and those followed in ours? We, too, trust above all the support found in treaties with friendly powers and armaments exceeding those of our potential enemies. We, too, pay verbal homage to God, while self-righteously pursuing our national interest without reference to his holy will. We praise the Lord and pass the ammunition. With few changes Isaiah's words apply to us:

> Woe to those who go to Europe for help,
>> and rely on jet planes,
> who trust in rockets because they are swift
>> and in hydrogen bombs because
>> they are very strong,
> but do not look to the Holy God of all mankind
>> or consult the Lord.
> The Europeans are men, and not God;
>> and their armies are flesh, and not
>> spirit.
> When the Lord stretches out his hand,
>> the makers of human alliances will
>> stumble and fall,
>> and they will all perish together.

Isaiah's counsel went unheeded. During the Syro-Ephraimite War, when Judah opposed him and sought the aid of Assyria, he had recorded his oracles as a testimony for the future. Now again, when the nation called on Egypt to help throw off Assyrian rule, he felt led by the Lord to write his message:

> And now, go, write it before them on a tablet,
>   and inscribe it in a book,
> that it may be for the time to come
>   as a witness forever (30:8).

Of such experiences the Book of Isaiah was born.

THE INVASION OF SENNACHERIB

Sennacherib moved swiftly to stamp out the revolts. After ousting Merodach-baladan from Babylon in 701 B.C. he turned to deal with Judah and other Palestinian states. Following quick successes in the north he reached Eltekeh, midway between Jerusalem and the Philistine city of Ekron. Here he decisively defeated the Ethiopian forces which had answered Ekron's appeal for help. Ekron had previously deposed its Assyrian king, Padi, asking Hezekiah to confine him in Jerusalem. The Assyrians now restored Padi to power and ruthlessly punished the rebels, killing their leaders and impaling their bodies on stakes. After a siege, Sennacherib captured the Judean city of Lachish, making it his headquarters for receiving tribute and the base of his operations against Hezekiah.

ISAIAH'S PHILOSOPHY OF HISTORY: As events unfolded Isaiah sought to interpret their meaning.

Assyria should be seen as the Lord's agent in chastising Judah for her sins. She was the rod of his anger, the staff of his fury, his ax for hewing down those who put themselves in his place, his saw for cutting off unhealthy boughs (10:5, 15, and 33-34). *Judah was called to the repentant endurance of divine discipline.*

This did not mean, however, that God approved of Assyria's conduct—quite the contrary! Sennacherib had no intention of advancing divine ends; he sought only the destruction of his enemies, conquest, plunder, glory. Even more than Judah, he had flouted the will of the Lord. He had claimed credit for accomplishments which only the power of God made possible, and had blasphemously imagined that the ax and the rod were superior to him who wielded them. When the discipline of Judah was complete, the king of Assyria would himself be punished (10:12-16). In this faith Isaiah counseled his countrymen not to lose heart, but to expect the time when the Lord would destroy Assyria and deliver Judah. After thundering among the nations, the conqueror would flee (10:24-27a; 17:12-14; 29:1-8). His downfall was sure.

The prophet's contemplation of the rise and fall of nations prepared him for a further revelation: *God's purposes embraced not only Judah and Assyria, but all peoples.* All history was subject to his rule, and nothing could thwart him.

"As I have purposed,
so shall it stand,

61

that I will break the Assyrian in my land,
    and upon my mountains trample him under foot;
and his yoke shall depart from them,
    and his burden from their shoulder."
This is the purpose that is purposed
    concerning the whole earth;
and this is the hand that is stretched out
    over all the nations. (14:24-27).

THE HUMILIATION OF JERUSALEM: Nevertheless,
dark days lay ahead for Judah. Sennacherib reports that he captured and plundered forty-six
walled towns, then shut up Hezekiah "like a caged
bird" in Jerusalem. Terrified, Hezekiah sent to
Lachish messengers who promised to meet any
conditions demanded for lifting the siege. In addition to her regular tribute, Judah was forced to
turn over to Sennacherib 300 talents of silver,
thirty talents of gold, and costly palace and temple
treasures, as well as the king's daughters, his
harem, and his male and female musicians. In spite
of the harshness of these terms, for some reason the
Assyrians did not enter Jerusalem.[1]

The apparent lifting of the siege sent the people
to the housetops in hilarious celebration. Long
pent-up emotions found expression in wild revelry.
For Isaiah, however, the occasion was one of
national disgrace. He could not forget the devastation which the Assyrians had wrought in the
land, isolating Jerusalem like a watchman's shelter
in a field after the harvest has left it a tangled mass

[1] The Hebrew and Assyrian accounts are in substantial agreement,
except that Sennacherib claims a levy of 800 talents of silver, probably
an exaggeration. See II Kings 18:13-16, and James B. Pritchard (ed.),
Ancient Near Eastern Texts Relating to the Old Testament, p. 288.

of withered vines (1:7-8). Only the Lord's mercy had made possible the survival of the capital.

Isaiah remembered also the sins which had brought the crisis, the flight of the pro-Egyptian leaders when their policy failed, the humiliation involved in the huge indemnity. In spite of these circumstances, the people were still blind to the hand of God in recent events, now as before trusting in themselves and paying much more attention to material and military defenses than to the divine purposes. Moreover, deadly dangers loomed ahead, "a day of tumult and trampling and confusion" which the people, living only in the present, refused to face. The situation should call forth solemn thanksgiving, weeping, and penitence. Instead, the people responded with empty-headed gaiety. Such practical atheism, preserved amid calamity with further disaster ahead, was unpardonable:

> In that day the Lord GOD of hosts,
>   called to weeping and mourning,
>   to baldness and girding with sackcloth;
> and behold, joy and gladness,
>   slaying oxen and killing sheep,
>   eating flesh and drinking wine.
> "Let us eat and drink,
>   for tomorrow we die."
> The LORD of hosts has revealed himself in my
>   ears;
> "Surely this iniquity will not be forgiven you
>   till you die" (22:12-14).

RENEWAL OF THE ASSYRIAN ATTACK: Apparently Sennacherib soon regretted leaving Jerusalem in Hezekiah's hands. Possibly he feared the consequences if he moved into an Egyptian campaign with the rebellious Judean king free to cause trouble in his rear. Accordingly, he sent his chief of staff and other officials, backed by a powerful armed force, to demand the surrender of the city. To meet them Hezekiah named Shebna his secretary, Eliakim his treasurer, and Joah his recorder. The encounter between the two delegations took place just outside the city wall.

Speaking in Hebrew, the Assyrians used three arguments to show the hopelessness of the Judean cause: (1) You still hope for Egyptian aid, but Egypt is a broken reed. (2) With neither chariots nor horsemen of your own, how can you hope to stand against our armed might? (3) You cannot count on help from your god, who was offended by your king's destruction of all his sanctuaries except the one in the capital.

Such arguments, hard to answer, might easily have undermined the morale of the city's defenders on the wall. Sensing this, the Judeans asked the spokesman to change to Aramaic, the language of diplomacy. Whereupon the Assyrian, stating that his message was really intended for the doomed citizens, continued in Hebrew more loudly than before. Hezekiah, he declared, is a deceiver, and cannot save you. Nor can Hezekiah's god, any more than the gods of the other nations already overrun by Sennacherib. If you surrender, you will be unharmed, and later enjoy new prosperity in another land like this.

The Judeans made no reply, but returned in

consternation to report to Hezekiah. The king tore his garments, covered himself with sackcloth, and went to the temple to lament and sacrifice before the Lord, meanwhile sending Eliakim, Shebna, and the elder priests to seek counsel from Isaiah.

THE SALVATION OF THE CITY: Though he had previously advised submission to the Assyrian demands, Isaiah now called for refusal. Sennacherib had clearly violated his agreement, and was overstepping the role assigned him and defying the will of God. So the prophet assured Hezekiah that there was nothing to fear, for the Lord "will put a spirit" in the king of Assyria, "so that he shall hear a rumor and return to his own land," there to meet death by the sword.[1]

This prediction was not based on military calculations or a realistic appraisal of the historical situation. All the external facts were against him. Judah lay helpless before the most powerful army in the world. Yet the prophet, discerning moral and spiritual realities that escaped the eye, dared to counsel against surrender. Confidently he asserted:

"Thus says the Lord concerning the king of Assyria: He shall not come into this city, or shoot an arrow there, or come before it with a shield, or cast up a siege-mound against it. By the way that he came, by the same he shall return, and he shall not come into this city, says the Lord. For I will

[1] This narrative is found in 36:1 through 37:7, a slight modification of II Kings 18:17 through 19:7. The account in 37:8-21, 33-35 and II Kings 19:8-20, 32-34 is probably a later independent version of the same events, though some students regard it as a description of a second threat, perhaps in 690.

defend this city to save it, for my own sake and for the sake of my servant David" (37:33-35; II Kings 19:32-34).

Encouraged by Isaiah's faith, Hezekiah refused to succumb, and the Assyrian officials were forced to return to their king with a negative report. In the meantime, rumors had spread of a northward advance by Tirhakah, the Ethiopian commander of the Egyptian army. Word came also of a new revolt of the Babylonians under Merodach-baladan. Apparently Sennacherib felt unable to cope with both threats at once, and began to withdraw from Palestine. His retreat was hastened when his troops were struck by what many students think was bubonic plague, and multitudes died. The account in 37:36-38 and II Kings 19:35-37 is legendary in form, exaggerating the size of the Assyrian army, the number of fatalities, and the speed of the disaster, but it contains a core of truth. Herodotus records an Egyptian story of an occasion when a swarm of mice at night devoured the bow-strings and shield-handles of an Assyrian army, so that they fled unarmed the next day, and many were killed. Believing that this story may refer to Sennacherib's campaign, some scholars find in it a possible explanation of the biblical narrative, since mice were an ancient Greek symbol of pestilence, and plague was carried by rats. Moreover, the Hebrew word for angel, *malak*, did not denote essentially a winged supernatural being, but simply an agent through which God's will was done (II Sam. 24:15-16).

At any rate, Sennacherib left Palestine. As stated in 37:38, he was also actually murdered by his sons, though not until twenty years later. Jerusalem was delivered without lifting a hand in its own defense. Events had confirmed the prophet's trust, powerfully supporting his claim to speak not the words of man, but the Word of God. An arrogant monarch had overreached himself. Judah was to be able for a century more to nurture and deepen the prophetic faith which proved her unique contribution to mankind.

VI

A KING WILL REIGN
IN RIGHTEOUSNESS

ISAIAH'S MESSIANIC PROPHECIES

Isaiah 2:2-5; 9:1-7;
11:1-9; 32:1-8, 15-18, 20

We HAVE purposely left unmentioned until now the "messianic" prophecies so familiar to and beloved by Christians. Unlike many of Isaiah's other utterances, these cannot be clearly related to known historical situations. The coronation of Ahaz or Hezekiah may have occasioned one or more of them. Some may have been written just after the deliverance of Jerusalem, when the prophet, about to retire finally from public life, turned with joy and hope to contemplate the future attainment of God's goal. Fortunately, the meaning of the passages does not depend on the time or manner of their origin. We shall therefore consider them together without any attempt to determine their dates.

For Christians, thought of the Messiah is so intimately connected with the coming of Jesus Christ that the precise meaning of the messianic hope for Jews in the eighth century B. C. is difficult to recapture. "The people that walked in darkness have seen a great light" reminds us instantly of the joyous advent season, or of a thrilling performance of Handel's *Messiah*. "Unto us a child is born" signifies for us one child only, the child of Bethlehem. But these hallowed associations make all the more important an appreciative understanding of the Jewish expectations from which they grew.

The messianic hope did not originate with Isaiah. He rather took it over, purged it of pagan elements, and gave it a distinctly ethical and spiritual quality. His portrayals of the messianic age are marked by freshness and diversity. Some passages stress the leadership of a personal messiah; others simply describe the kingdom itself. Some picture a deeply religious community, others a political state. Some look mainly for a new order in human relations; others extend this to the whole realm of nature. Isaiah's ideas varied with his mood, but through them all shore brightly his confident belief that God would fulfill his holy purpose for Judah and the world.

THE CHARACTER OF THE RULER: Particularly in 9:6-7 and 11:1-5 Isaiah depicts the character of the ruler. Since Israel's greatest glory had been reached under the reign of David, before Solomon's tyranny had divided the kingdom, patriotic Jews naturally focused their dreams of a new Israel on some descendant of David. The coronation of every king of the Davidic line aroused new hope for the restoration of vanished grandeur and the attainment of greater heights. Each was anointed in a religious rite and thenceforth regarded as an agent of God—in a sense a sacred person, set apart for a special function. Out of this rite grew the custom of describing the expected ideal king as *mashiah*— anointed one—anglicized as Messiah.[1] In this sense the king portrayed by Isaiah may be properly referred to as messianic, though the prophet himself does not use the term.

The names applied to the expected king— "Wonderful Counselor, Mighty God, Everlasting Father, Prince of Peace"—suggest an almost superhuman being. Actually, they designate not a king who is himself divine, but one who, because he is endowed for his task by the Lord, is the human embodiment of God's kingship. "Mighty God" means "Godlike hero," one who is "divine in might," gifted with extraordinary power and insight because the Spirit of God dwells within him. "Everlasting Father" means "Father-forever," the stress being on the constancy of the ruler's fatherly care for his people. The four names in chapter 9 have the same basic meaning as the inspired words of chapter 11:

> The Spirit of the LORD shall rest upon him,
> the spirit of wisdom and understanding,
> the spirit of counsel and might,
> the spirit of knowledge and the fear of the LORD.

Such a ruler will not judge by appearances, but

---

[1] Since *mashiah* usually referred to a king, any promise of a king was in a broad sense messianic.

according to truth and justice. He will thwart the wicked and uphold the poor and lowly. In righteousness and faithfulness will be his strength.

THE NATURE OF THE KINGDOM: Isaiah devotes even more attention to the nature of the kingdom. In 2:2-5, found also in Micah 4:1-4, he makes no reference to a king, but paints a glowing picture of a time when all peoples will look to Jerusalem as their religious center. There they will learn from the God of Jacob how to live together in harmony. Yet there is no hint of Jewish domination. Significantly, "the house of the Lord" is not described as a place where ritualistic acts are performed, but as a center where the divine will is revealed. The Lord himself will settle disputes between the nations;

> and they shall beat their swords into plowshares,
> and their spears into pruning hooks;
> nation shall not lift up sword against nation,
> neither shall they learn war any more.[1]

In chapter 32 there is a brief reference to a king who "will reign in righteousness," and to the sturdy character of the princes who will assist him. Then major attention is directed to the noble, ordered living of ordinary citizens, all of whom are, as it were, anointed: "the Spirit is poured upon us from on high." The first Christians at Pentecost recognized just such an outpouring of the divine Spirit as the sign of a new age (Acts 2:1-18, 33). For Isaiah, too, it means a new society.

[1] The poem is more complete if Micah 4:4 is added here. See also Zechariah 3:10.

71

in which the effect of righteousness will be peace, and "quietness and trust for ever."

In the first part of chapter 9 the prophet projects himself into the future and imagines the ideal age as already realized. Darkness has been transformed into light. The people are filled with joy, for they have been freed from oppression and war, and they have been given a divinely endowed king. The description of the government makes no mention of material prosperity, expanded territory, or mighty armies. It will be upheld rather

> with justice and with righteousness
> from this time forth and for evermore.

Only such a kingdom, supported by "the zeal of the LORD of hosts," can really endure. In our time we have seen another state, founded on racial pride, hatred, suppression of freedom, and colossal armaments. It was led by Adolph Hitler, who rejected the Old Testament as a Jewish book, and who boasted that his government would endure for a millennium. It lasted twelve years.

The prophecy in 11:1-9 broadens the ideal reign to include even the animal world and man's relation to it. Isaiah envisions a time when domestic and wild beasts will live amicably together, and when infants may play without danger near the holes of poisonous snakes. However naive this may sound if taken literally, it truly symbolizes God's concern for all that he has made. Perhaps it may give us also something of Albert Schweitzer's "reverence for life," so that we shall kill and use animals only when necessary and with deep regret, living so as to advance and enrich other life with the strength gained from the life destroyed. God's loving purpose embraces the whole creation. When men become aware of this, truly

> they shall not hurt or destroy
> in all my holy mountain;
> for the earth shall be full of the knowledge
> of the LORD
> as the waters cover the sea.

THE FULFILLMENT OF THE PROPHECIES: Clearly these prophecies did not specifically predict the coming of Jesus of Nazareth. However, in the deepest sense they were fulfilled in him. As the generations passed, no leader appeared who even approximated Isaiah's picture of the Anointed One. But after the last king of Judah had died an exile in Babylon, the hope persisted that God would yet send a Davidic king to lead his people into a new age. Enriched and deepened by Second Isaiah, that hope was cherished in the long baffling centuries of struggle and subjection, until finally a Redeemer appeared who exceeded Isaiah's fondest dreams.

"When the time had fully come, God sent forth his son" (Gal. 4:4). The expectation long treasured by the prophets prepared the way for Jesus, truly the Anointed One. Isaiah had spoken better than he knew. The ideal earthly king has never come, but the Christ who has come displays a truer royalty. The perfect earthly state remains a dream, but God has founded in Jesus Christ a spiritual community of love and righteousness which makes all things new.

ISAIAH'S RELIGIOUS TEACHINGS

We have followed Isaiah through the forty years of his prophetic activity, considering his various utterances in connection with the critical events which called them forth. We shall understand him and his meaning for our lives still better if we now try to see his religious teachings as a whole. Reappearing throughout his ministry, from his temple vision to the deliverance of Jerusalem, are five main ideas. His message is a tapestry woven of five threads.

1. THE HOLINESS OF GOD: Central to Isaiah's thinking and living is his awareness of God as holy—as a being of transcendent majesty and awful power. Holiness is the very essence of deity. Negatively, it indicates the ineffable otherness of God, the decisive separation between him and his creatures. Positively, it suggests all the attributes of God which arouse awe, reverence, and adoration.

Within the context of this generally held belief Isaiah adds two important emphases of his own. First, the *divine holiness is essentially ethical.* God is high and lifted up not only in wisdom and might, but in goodness. In his presence man feels not only finite and creaturely but sinful, because he stands before absolute moral perfection. "The Holy God shows himself holy in righteousness" (5:16; see 5:24; 6:1-8).

Secondly, *for Isaiah the holiness of God is related to the peculiar needs and responsibilities of the people who worship him*. He gives to the Holy One a new title: the Holy One *of Israel* (10:20; 30:15; 31:1). The name occurs eleven times in chapters 1 through 31, and is taken over and used thirteen times in chapters 41 through 60; outside of this book it appears only five times in the entire Old Testament. By adding two words, Isaiah bridges the gap between the awesome grandeur of the Most High and the aspirations of men. God's holiness does not mean remoteness from human interests or indifference to human need. It is tempered by personal concern for the "sons" whom he has "reared and brought up" (1:2, 4). He is the Holy One of Israel. But since he alone is God, and since all nations are subject to his will, he is also the Holy One of all peoples who recognize his rule. Is he the Holy One of America?

2. THE RIGHTEOUS JUDGMENT OF GOD: The holy God who is supremely righteous requires ethical character in his worshipers. Ritual is not an end in itself, but a means whereby men express their adoration of God and their devotion to him. It is empty unless accompanied by a life dedicated to God's will. Not only is the Lord exalted in righteousness, but men exalt him in their hearts by living righteously.

Inevitably, those who flout the will of God place themselves under his righteous judgment (1:20-31; 2:12-19; 3:16 through 4:1; 5:1-24; 9:8 through 10:4; 28:14-22). His goodness is firm and uncompromising. His world is a moral order, in which we reap as we sow. We are free to try living life on our own terms. But like the supersonic Navy jet plane which, speeding at 880 miles per hour, caught up with cannon shells it had fired and shot itself down,[1] we only accomplish our own ruin. Soon or late we learn the bitter truth of James Weldon Johnson's lines addressed to the prodigal son:

Young man—
Your arm's too short to box with God.[2]

The exploitation of others and indifference to their welfare cuts us off from our fellow men, without whom our lives are not complete. Self-indulgence and the effort to accumulate material goods blind us to the really important values. Pride in our own wisdom, trust in our own strength, belief in our own goodness—whether national or individual—all are forms of idolatry which effectively separate us from God. Yet only in God is our true life to be found.

3. God's Control over History: Implied in God's judgment of men and nations is his lordship over history. Just as his glory fills the whole earth, so his purpose pervades all human events. That purpose will be consummated in a "day of the Lord" which will bring the overthrow of evil and the triumph of God's righteousness.

So great is God's power and so subtle his wisdom that he uses even evil men and movements to attain his ends. "Surely the wrath of man shall praise thee," sings the Psalmist (Psa. 76:10), and

[1] *The Boston Globe*, October 26, 1956.
[2] *God's Trombones* (New York: Viking Press, 1927), p. 21. Used by permission.

Isaiah agrees. Though Sennacherib "does not so intend, and his mind does not so think," his selfish exploits become in God's hands a means of disciplining the Hebrews and awakening in them a sense of their true destiny (Isa. 10:5-16). But he himself must reckon with the Lord of history, whose moral law makes evil finally self-defeating. Man's evil eventually confronts one who says, "It shall not stand, and it shall not come to pass" (7:7; see 30:1-17, 27-33; 31:1-5).

Recent events as well as those in the more distant past witness to the truth of Isaiah's teaching. Amid a growing awareness that the use of hydrogen bombs in warfare may mean the end of life on this planet, there are faint signs that men may be urged partly by this awareness to find non-violent ways of settling international disputes. If on the other hand we go on to blow ourselves to bits, even this grim outcome will demonstrate our incapacity to build an enduring civilization on our own man-centered terms.

Another aspect of Isaiah's thought becomes especially relevant here. Observing the plight of the people of Jerusalem, barely surviving amid the devastation wrought by the "scorched earth" measures of the invader, yet still unrepentant, he reflects that it is only by the grace of God that they remain alive at all (1:4-9). *Behind history is the mercy of God.* It does not cancel his judgment, but it repeatedly extends to men undeserved opportunities to turn from those ways that provoke judgment. R. B. Y. Scott writes truly: "Only by

the mercy of God whose goodness we have spurned
and whose moral law we have disobeyed do we
survive to learn the lesson of history—that the
desolation we lament is the direct result of our
own moral failure."[1] How well we learn that lesson
may determine how long we survive.

4. MAN'S CENTRAL NEED FOR FAITH: With human destiny ultimately in the hands of a holy,
righteous God, man's basic need is faith in God.
This is Isaiah's reliance in each new political
crisis: "In quietness and in trust shall be your
strength" (30:15; 7:4, 9; 18:4; 28:12, 16). This
is his resource as he faces personal failure: "I will
wait for the Lord . . . and I will hope in him"
(8:17). Our highest purposes are grounded in a
sovereign goodness at the heart of the world. How
foolish, then—and how faithless—to ignore God
and trust instead in frail human devices!

The center of religion is quiet yet active confidence in the power and wisdom of God. For Isaiah
faith is far more than intellectual belief. It is trust
in the unseen but decisive activity of him on whom
everything ultimately depends. To trust God
means to yield our lives to his keeping and to commit ourselves obediently to his steadfast righteous
will. Only such faith affords an adequate foundation for a stable and just society.

We can understand even better what faith means
for Isaiah if we look at its reverse. Actually he
mentions two opposites. One of them is pride,
man's conceited belief in his own sufficiency, his

[1] *The Interpreter's Bible*, V, 170.

reliance on his own wisdom and strength. The other is fear, the anxiety which quails before any threat to his cherished enterprises. The connection is not accidental. He who trusts nothing higher than himself—or than man—has no defense against the evils that strike terror to the human heart. Fear in turn encourages the self-conceit which pretends not to be afraid. The answer to both is faith in him who alone is worthy of our supreme devotion. As George Neumark sings,

> Who trusts in God's unchanging love
> Builds on the rock that naught can move.[1]

5. GROUNDS OF HOPE: The depth of Isaiah's personal faith gives him also grounds for hope. Though divine judgment on human evil bulks large in his message, its basic purpose is not destruction but purification. Persistence in sin brings disaster, but God seeks through disciplining his people to lead them to repentance and obedience (1:25-26; 9:13; 10:12). Hence there is hope for Judah and for mankind. Isaiah's gospel of hope has two foci: *the messianic kingdom* and *the faithful remnant.* Both root in God. However, the former depends overwhelmingly on divine action, while the latter waits on men's humble, trustful response (1:19). The messianic hope has already been discussed in this chapter. The idea of the remnant needs further comment.

Though Isaiah expects the nation as a whole to reject his message and go down to ruin, he looks

---

[1] *The Methodist Hymnal,* No. 272. Translated by Catherine Wink worth.

for the emergence of a faithful few through whom renewal will come when the crisis is past. "Out of Jerusalem will go forth a remnant, and out of Mount Zion a band of survivors," who "will lean upon the Lord . . . in truth" (37:32; 1:9, 26; 6:13; 7:3; 10:20-22; 11:16; 28:5). Because of the cleansing, renewing action of God, the original warning that *only* a remnant will turn to the Lord becomes a promise that a remnant *will* turn. Isaiah finds the nucleus of this redemptive fellowship in the little band of his own disciples to whom he commits "the teaching and the testimony." In this committed group, empowered by God, lies his hope for the future.

Again and again in history the church has been such a remnant. When it has failed, becoming too much like the world around it, repeatedly it has been itself renewed by a faithful remnant within. Today the church is called to be God's agent in the renewal of men and the rebirth and transformation of society. Does it instead too largely reflect the pride, the fears, and the ethical standards of the world at large? Then its chief hope for rebirth, humanly speaking, is through the influence of little cells of faithful, Spirit-filled men and women.

Part Three

ISAIAH,
CHAPTERS 40 THROUGH 55

VII

COMFORT, MY PEOPLE

THE NATURE OF CHAPTERS 40 THROUGH 66

WHEN the attentive student of the Book of Isaiah passes from the historical narrative of chapter 39 to the noble poems which begin with chapter 40, he becomes aware of a changed situation. Destruction and exile are not predicted for the future, but are present realities. The writer implies that Jerusalem, as well as the other cities of Judah, has been destroyed (44:26). The Hebrew people have been widely scattered (43:5-6). They are enduring humiliation and suffering as captives in Babylon (40:2; 42:7, 22; 47:5; 48:20; 49:9; 51:23), which is now the dominant world power. A new conqueror, Cyrus, is already on the march, and will soon overthrow Babylon (44:28; 46:1-2; 47; 48:14). These prophecies are clearly addressed to a people in exile. In addition, as indicated on pages 8-9, there are also marked differences in language, literary style, and religious ideas between these chapters and the prophecies of Isaiah of Jerusalem.

There is also weighty evidence that chapters 40 through 66 are themselves made up of two main sections, 40 through 55 and 56 through 66, produced by different authors at different times. The two parts do contain many similarities in language, style, and thought, and they resemble each other much more than either resembles the writings of Isaiah himself. Nevertheless, there are notable differences. Beginning with chapter 56, there is a stress on the outward aspects of religion, such as the temple ritual, sabbath observance, and fasting, that is largely missing from chapters 40 through 55. Though the Jewish community seems largely free from external control, its efforts to provide pure forms of worship are hampered by discord. The geography is not Babylonian but Palestinian. There is less hopefulness regarding the future than in the preceding passages. Though chapters 40 through 55 are thoroughly universalistic in their outlook, chapters 56 through 66 are more nationalistic. In the latter, foreigners are accepted but given a subordinate role; Israel is called less to service than to lordship (60:1-14; 61:5).

Circumstances like these suggest two important conclusions:

(1) Chapters 40 through 55 are the work of a prophet-poet writing near the close of the Babylonian captivity, about 540 B.C.[1]

(2) Chapters 56 through 66 were written after

[1] Chapters 34 and 35 may have served at one time as an introduction to this work. Following the announcement of the fearful judgment of God in chapter 34, chapter 35 is a joyful proclamation of divine deliverance closely akin to that in chapters 40-55.

the return of the exiles to Palestine, and reflect
the difficult problems involved in reconstruction
and the restoration of temple worship.[1]

THE HISTORICAL BACKGROUND
OF CHAPTERS 40 THROUGH 55

The kingdom of Judah survived more than a
century after the deliverance of Jerusalem in 701
B.C. During this time Assyria extended its conquests to include Egypt, while Judah continued in
subjection. However, toward the end of the century, Assyrian power declined until, in 612 B.C.,
Nineveh fell before the onslaught of the Medes and
Babylonians under Esarhaddon of Babylon. What
had been the Assyrian Empire was divided between two powers, Media in the north and Babylonia in the south.

The exchange of masters left Judah's position
unimproved. Forced to pay tribute to Babylonia,
she rebelled at the first opportunity. The resultant
invasions by Nebuchadnezzar (605-562 B.C.) led to
the complete destruction of Jerusalem in 587 B.C.
and a series of deportations which carried a total
of 4,600 Judeans into captivity in Babylon (Jer. 32:
1-2; 52:1-30; II Kings 25:8-26). Isaiah's prediction was thus finally fulfilled. The kingdom of
Judah, and with it the Davidic line of kings, came
to an ignoble end. With their temple a heap of
rubble and their homeland in ruins, the captives
began the long years of exile on foreign soil.

[1] The first conclusion has overwhelming acceptance among scholars.
The second is held by a majority, though a strong minority maintain the
unity of chapters 40 through 66. See *The Interpreter's Bible*, V, 383, n.13.

The division of power which followed the downfall of Assyria proved quite unstable. Though for more than half a century an uneasy balance was preserved, the situation changed with the appearance of Cyrus, vigorous young king of Elam in Persia. In a three-year campaign opening in 553 B.C., Cyrus overthrew Astyages (584-550 B.C.) and replaced him as ruler of Media, thereby laying the foundation of the Medo-Persian Empire which dominated the Near East for over 200 years. In 546 B.C. Cyrus became king of Persia. In 540 B.C. he defeated Croesus, the fabulously wealthy king of Lydia, and soon overran Asia Minor. In 539 B.C. he turned toward Babylon, which was ripe for conquest. Nabonidus (556-538 B.C.) had already lost the confidence of his people and the support of the powerful priests by his rejection of the official cult of Marduk and his worship of the ancient moon-god. Cyrus defeated the Babylonians at Opis, precipitating a revolt, and the way to Babylon itself lay open. Led by a deserted Babylonian officer, the Persians diverted the Tigris River from its channel and used the shallow river bed to enter the walled city. By means of this brilliant maneuver, on October 13, 539 B.C. they occupied Babylon without a struggle.

The beginning of Persian rule brought the Jewish captivity to an end. One of Cyrus' first acts was to issue a decree (538 B.C.) allowing the various peoples held captive in Babylon to return to their homes. He attributed his victory to the favor of Marduk, and perhaps felt that Marduk was angered by the fact that the foreign gods of the captives had been given homes in his sacred city. In any event, the inscription on the cylinder of Cyrus reports: "I returned to (these) sacred cities on the other side of the Tigris, the sanctuaries of which have been in ruins for a long time, the images which (used) to live therein and established for them permanent sanctuaries. I (also) gathered all their (former) inhabitants and returned (to them) their habitations . . . all of them I settled in a peaceful place."[1]

The biblical account of the decree relates it particularly to the Jews. Though it naturally assigns ultimate rule to God rather than Marduk, it agrees with the cylinder regarding the historical facts: "The Lord stirred up the spirit of Cyrus king of Persia so that he made a proclamation throughout all his kingdom and also put it in writing:

"Thus says Cyrus king of Persia: The Lord, the God of heaven, has given me all the kingdoms of the earth, and he has charged me to build him a house at Jerusalem, which is in Judah, and rebuild the house of the Lord, the God of Israel" (Ezra 1:1-3; II Chron. 36:22-23). In 537 B.C. the first of the returning exiles undertook the difficult journey back to Jerusalem.

THE LIFE OF THE EXILES

From various sources we know a good deal about the conditions faced by the exiles. Some in-

[1] James B. Pritchard (ed.), *Ancient Near Eastern Texts Relating to the Old Testament*, p. 316. Used by permission.

formation can of course be derived from Second Isaiah—the name usually given to the author of chapters 40 through 55. Further insight is offered by statements of Jeremiah and Ezekiel, whose prophetic ministries extended into the exilic period. Ezekiel is especially helpful, since he was himself one of the exiles. Several of the Psalms, notably 42, 129, 130, and 137, reflect the mood of the captives.

The Jews in Babylon were apparently not persecuted. They were granted the use of the land, and many tilled the soil. Gradually some became occupied in business and trade. Many lived in their own houses (Jer. 29:5). They were granted the right of assembly, and many met regularly for religious purposes. Such small gatherings may have been the origin of the Jewish synagogue.

Since the temple and the religious institutions connected with it were gone, other forms of expression were stressed. Sabbath observance grew in importance. New meaning was discovered in prayer. The people cherished old memories and traditions, preserving continuity with the faith of their ancestors by recalling the Mosaic covenant and the lives and teachings of the prophets:

> By the waters of Babylon, there we sat
>   down and wept,
>   when we remembered Zion (Psa. 137:1).

Though they went on to lament,

>   How shall we sing the LORD's song
>   in a foreign land?

they nevertheless found comfort and inspiration in hymns and other sacred songs.[1]

Naturally they became somewhat adjusted to their new life as the years wore on. Also, a generation gradually grew up to whom Babylon was home, and who had no particular desire to move to Palestine. Developments like these posed knotty religious problems. The Babylonian cults exerted a powerful influence. Some of them were highly sensual, and their color and pageantry appealed to people living the drab life of exiles. The further fact that Babylon was a victorious military power no doubt tempted many to adopt Babylonian religious observances to secure the help of the mighty Marduk.

In spite of their adjustment to life in Babylon, many of the exiles were at heart perplexed and despondent. Unable to understand the catastrophe which had destroyed their homes and forcibly transported them 600 miles to the land of their conqueror, they doubted the goodness or the power of God, who had permitted such suffering. Those who yearned to return to Palestine wondered whether their God was really able to deliver them. Even the rumors of the rise of Cyrus aroused alarm. Having attained a certain orderliness and stability in their existence, they were distressed by the uncertainty and the threat of change which his conquests produced. They searched their hearts as to what new and possibly worse fate might be in

[1] An excellent way to feel the mood of the exiles, voiced in Psalm 137, is to listen receptively to Johann Sebastian Bach's beautiful chorale prelude, "By the Waters of Babylon."

store for them if Cyrus captured Babylon. To such a people burdened with such questions the unknown prophet of the exile was called to minister.

THE POET-PROPHET AND HIS POEMS

THE AUTHOR: We know nothing about the personal life of the author of Isaiah 40 through 55. Not only his own name, but those of his parents, the place and date of his birth, and the locale of his ministry are shrouded in mystery. He is so familiar with conditions in Babylon (44:24-25; 47:12-13) and refers to it so frequently that Babylon is the most likely location; though Palestine, Phoenicia, and Egypt have all been suggested. Nor do we know for what occasions his messages were composed, to whom they were addressed, or whether or not he spoke as well as wrote them. Apparently for him the task of hearing and proclaiming the word of God for his day was so momentous, and the scope of the divine purpose so vast, that he allowed himself to fade completely into the background.

Nevertheless, the poems tell us much about the character of the author. He appears to have been the spiritual leader of the exiles. In feeling and in thought he was equally profound. His sympathies were universal, embracing mankind, the animal world, and all nature. He was capable of deep anger and of even deeper compassion. A gifted poet as well as an inspired prophet, he broke forth in song in which the dominant notes were grace and hope. Above all he was a man of God, overwhelmed by his experience of God's suffering and universal love, and eager to proclaim his evangel to Israel and the world.

The poems tell us something also about their original form of presentation. The marks of literary craftsmanship and orderly arrangement are so unmistakable that they must have been written before being spoken. However, they may have been delivered in gatherings of exiles, perhaps on the Sabbath during worship, or sent to other groups for reading aloud. In such fashion their message of correction, comfort, and hope would reach best those who needed it most.

THE MESSAGE OF THE POEMS: The poems are marked by both independence and interrelatedness. They represent varying moods and suggest various background occasions. A division between chapters 40 through 48 and 49 through 55 is plainly observable; in the latter chapters there is no reference to Cyrus, and some emphases of the former are missing. Yet the similarities in style and content far exceed the differences. Whether or not the poems were originally separate units, they have been woven together with such literary artistry that they form a rounded whole.

The opening and closing poems (40:1-11; 55:1-13) are connected by common threads of thought which also interpenetrate the fabric of the intervening songs. Many major themes recur: the infinity of God, who is both Creator of the world and Lord of history; the non-existence of other gods the coming deliverance and restoration of Israel; the role of Cyrus; God's purpose to redeem all nations; the mission of Israel; the suffering servant. Even more significant is the movement of the prophet's thought. The poems really comprise a great drama which advances from the initial announcement of the Lord's coming with power to the exultant climax proclaiming the accomplishment of the divine purposes. The drama heralds a momentous divine event which will bring the old age to a decisive end and inaugurate a new one. Chapters 40 through 48 treat the imminent coming of God; chapters 49 through 55, the redemption of Israel and all nations.[1]

Lofty themes like these require the skilled treatment of a master-poet, a profound thinker, and an inspired prophet. All these they find in Second Isaiah, who is equally at home whether depicting the matchless power or the tender compassion of God, his judgment or his grace. Here Hebrew prophecy reaches its highest peak and makes its sublimest disclosures of the Eternal.

Though the poet speaks primarily to the needs of the Hebrew exiles, his perspective is universal. God's activity extends to the whole world and embraces all time. He works mightily in three great areas: creation, history, and redemption. Redemption is central, but it cannot be separated from creation, nor can either be understood apart from the events which connect them. The end must

[1] For an excellent detailed outline, see James Muilenburg's Introduction to Isaiah 40-66, *The Interpreter's Bible*, V, 415-418.

be related to the beginning, and the two are linked by history. God's action is decisive in all three; he is Creator, Lord of history, and Redeemer. To these emphases the prophet adds a fourth: the fulfillment of God's saving purpose through the voluntary suffering of his "servant."

The central message of Second Isaiah to Israel may therefore be summarized in four affirmations which will be developed in our next four chapters:

1. Your God is the sole Creator and Sustainer of all nature, and you are in his care.

2. All the events of history, including the destiny of Israel, are subject to his control.

3. God is about to act decisively to deliver and redeem Israel, and to bring all nations eventually to himself.

4. The suffering of God's servant, willingly borne for others, will be instrumental in redeeming both creation and history, thus consummating the divine purpose. Israel herself has a sacred mission.

We modern exiles shall do well to listen to the prophet attentively. Like those to whom he first wrote, we, too, may through his message find our way home.

VIII

TO WHOM WILL YOU
LIKEN GOD?

A PERPLEXED PEOPLE

Second Isaiah's first word to his perplexed and downhearted people is a joyous proclamation of pardon and deliverance: "Comfort, my people . . . . Behold, the Lord God comes with might." They have already suffered beyond their deserts, their time of service is over, and their release is at hand. The power of Babylon is but human, and like all flesh, it is perishable, while the purpose of God stands fast. In the wilderness is being prepared a highway over which their triumphant God will lead them with the tenderness of a shepherd (40:1-11).

Apparently the exiles did not at first share the prophet's exultation. Dulled by years of resignation and torn by doubts, they were not easily consoled, let alone stirred to enthusiasm. Perhaps their God did not really care, and maybe Bel and Nebo were after all more powerful than the Lord (40:27; 46:1; 49:14). For people in this mood a mere prediction of release was not enough. Their fundamental religious convictions needed to be clarified and corrected. They needed to learn the truth about the ultimate nature of the world in which they were having such a hard time. The poet goes straight to the heart of the matter. In impassioned stanzas he sings of the sole existence and the matchless power and wisdom of God.

THE INCOMPARABLE GOD

THE WORLD'S DEPENDENCE ON GOD: Emphatically Second Isaiah declares that the Lord alone is the Creator and Sustainer of the universe. The verb *to create* appears sixteen times in chapters 40 through 55, while equivalents like *make* and *form* appear with similar frequency. Only God can perform the creative act and bring into being what did not exist before.

> I am the LORD, who made all things,
>> who stretched out the heavens alone,
>> who spread out the earth—Who was with me?
>
> . . . .
>
> Lift up your eyes on high and see:
>> who created these?
> He who brings out their host by number,
>> calling them all by name (44:24; 40:26).

Nature is not a self-running mechanism. It is rather dependent on and responsive to the will of God. When he "calls" to the heavenly bodies, "they stand forth together" (48:13). In the graphic words of G. K. Chesterton, the sun does not rise "merely as the result of the earth's motion. It rises because God says, 'Get up!' "[1]

[1] Quoted in Paul Scherer, *Event in Eternity*, (New York: Harper & Bros., 1945), p. 36. Used by permission.

THE ETERNAL RULER OF MEN AND NATIONS: But the physical world is not an end in itself; it is instrumental to the creation and salvation of people whom God cherishes. The Lord "gives breath to the people" on the earth and "spirit to those who walk in it." He did not create the earth "a chaos," but "formed it to be inhabited" (42:5; 45:8, 18; see 45:12). Creation has an end: the fulfillment of God's purposes for his creatures.

Yet men are still creatures, and none can usurp the place of his Creator. Even the most powerful rulers are as nothing in contrast to him on whom their very existence depends.

> Behold, the nations are like a drop from a bucket,
>   and are accounted as the dust on the scales;
>
> . . . .
>
> All the nations are as nothing before him,
>   they are accounted by him as less than
>   nothing and emptiness.
>
> . . . .
>
> It is he who sits above the circle of the earth,
>   and its inhabitants are like grasshoppers;
> who stretches out the heavens like a curtain,
>   and spreads them like a tent to dwell in;
> who brings princes to nought,
>   and makes the rulers of the earth as nothing
>   (40:15-17, 21-25).

The Lord is as wise as he is powerful, and in relation to him men are as foolish as they are weak. How hopelessly inadequate are our best human devices for measuring the vastness of nature! Imagine trying to mark off the heavens with a span (the distance between the extended thumb and little finger of one's hand), or computing the

earth's volume with a peck measure, or weighing
the mountains with a jeweler's scales!

> Who has directed the Spirit of the LORD,
>   or as his counselor has instructed him?
> Whom did he consult for his enlightenment,
>   and who taught him the path of justice,
> and taught him knowledge,
>   and showed him the way of understanding?
>   (40:12-14).

A similar contrast obtains between the finitude
and mortality of man and the eternity of God.
"All flesh is grass," and grass withers before the
breath of the Lord. Princes, no more durable than
other men, also wilt before the winds of God, "and
the tempest carries them off like stubble" (40:6-8,
24). But the Lord is "the first and with the last"
(41:4; 44:6; 48:12), the beginning and the end
of our human existence, "the everlasting God"
(40:28) who is Lord of time and fulfills his purpose in time. To him we appropriately pray:

> Change and decay in all around I see;
> O Thou, who changest not, abide with me.[1]

THE KEEPER OF ISRAEL: It is this eternal God of
majestic wisdom and power who controls the destinies of Israel and other nations. Why should
Israel quake with fear?

> "I, I am he that comforts you;
>   who are you that you are afraid of man who dies,
>   of the son of man who is made like grass,
> and have forgotten the LORD, your Maker?
>
> . . . .
>
> and fear continually all the day
>   because of the fury of the oppressor?

[1] *The Methodist Hymnal*, No. 520.

97

. . . .
I have put my words in your mouth,
    and hid you in the shadow of my hand,
  stretching out the heavens
    and laying the foundations of the earth,
    and saying to Zion, 'You are my people' "
      (51:12-16).

In the keeping of such a God Israel may face the future in confidence. He rules in Babylon as well as in Palestine. His purposes will prevail as surely as rain and snow water the earth, help plants to grow, and provide food for men:

"So shall my word be that goes forth from my
      mouth;
    it shall not return to me empty,
  but it shall accomplish that which I purpose,
    and prosper in the thing for which I sent it"
      (55:10-11; see 46:10).

THE NONEXISTENCE OF OTHER GODS

ONLY ONE GOD: Clearly implied in the incomparable majesty of the eternal God is the falsity of all belief in other gods, which are nothing.

"I am God, and there is no other;
    I am God, and there is none like me (46:9).
  Before me no god was formed,
    nor shall there be any after me.
  I, I am the LORD,
    and besides me there is no savior" (43:10-11).

Cyrus may think he is the agent of Marduk. Actually, he is commissioned and empowered by the Lord, who addresses him:

"For the sake of my servant Jacob,
    and Israel my chosen,
  I call you by your name,

I surname you, though you do not know me.
I am the LORD, and there is no other,
    besides me there is no God;
I gird you, though you do not know me,
that men may know, from the rising of the sun
    and from the west, that there is none
        besides me;
I am the LORD, and there is no other" (45:4-6).

The time will come when other nations will themselves recognize the illusoriness of their own faith. For example, the people of Egypt, Ethiopia, and Sheba will confess to Israel:

"God is with you only, and there is no other,
no god besides him"
    (45:14; see 44:6; 45:18).

FORETELLER OF THE FUTURE: In proof of his denial that heathen gods exist, Second Isaiah frequently points out that the Lord alone can foretell future events. A major reason for this predictive activity of God is his desire to forestall those who, after certain events occur, credit idols with causing them.

"Before they came to pass I announced
    them to you,
lest you should say, 'My idol did them,
    my graven image and my molten image
      commanded them' " (48:3-5).

Actually, "the former things" predicted through God's prophets have taken place, and he now declares "new things" before they spring forth (42:9; 46:10). Can any other being do this? If so, "let him proclaim it." The challenge is hurled to all alleged deities: "Set forth your case . . . ; bring your proofs." Let them list the past events which

99

they foretold, and tell us what is to happen, so that we may know they are really gods. Hearing no answer, the poet invites the non-existent gods to do anything to demonstrate their reality:

> Do good, do harm,
>> that we may be dismayed and terrified.

There is no response, and the conclusion is clear:

> Behold, you are nothing,
>> and your work is nought;
>> an abomination is he who chooses you
>>> (44:7-8; 41:21-24).

Exhibit A in the prophet's gallery of proofs is the approach of Cyrus, whom God "stirred up from the north," and whose conquests he foretold. But no other god even claims to have predicted this. "They are all a delusion," their molten images "but empty wind" (41:25-29).

THE FOOLISHNESS OF IDOL-WORSHIP: How foolish, then, is the manufacture and worship of idols! In biting satire the prophet describes the craftsmen who are so ignorant that they fashion images with their own hands and then, with no sense of incongruity, bow down and worship them. The carpenter uses half a tree for firewood to warm himself and cook his food, then shapes the other part into an idol. Falling down before this block of wood he prays, "Deliver me, for thou art my god!" Poor, deceived man! "A deluded mind has led him astray" (44:9-20).

"To whom then will you liken God?" However skilled the workman or precious the metal, an image formed by man cannot even move (40:18-20;

46:5-7). How then can it aid its worshipers? Expecting the early fall of Babylon, the poet visualizes the flight of its citizens. They load their idols, Bel-Marduk and Nebo, the son of Marduk, on beasts in order to carry them away. What a strange reversal! They are forced to rescue their gods instead of being rescued by them (46:1-2). Yet such a predicament always results when the true God is replaced by unreal imitations (42:17).

On the contrary, those who trust in the Lord have no ultimate ground for fear. He is the eternal Creator and Sustainer of the whole world; all things are under his wise and righteous rule. In his power his worshipers, too, are strong. In a glowing climax the poet relates his momentous revelation directly to the questionings of the exiles.

> Why do you say, O Jacob,
>> and speak, O Israel.
> "My way is hid from the LORD,
>> and my right is disregarded by my God"?
> Have you not known? Have you not heard?
> The LORD is the everlasting God,
>> the Creator of the ends of the earth.
> He does not faint or grow weary,
>> his understanding is unsearchable.
> He gives power to the faint,
>> and to him who has no might he increases
>>> strength.
> Even youths shall faint and be weary,
>> and young men shall fall exhausted;
> but they who wait for the LORD shall renew their
>> strength,
>> they shall mount up with wings like eagles,
> they shall run and not be weary,
>> they shall walk and not faint (40:27-31).

WHAT ABOUT OURSELVES?

Though Second Isaiah wrote 2,500 years ago, his message is as relevant today as then. How many of us really share his world-embracing faith? We stamp on our coins, "In God we trust"; and in theory we worship the Lord of all being. Yet is not the god we really serve often a nationalistic or racial deity whom we trust to bless our narrow aims, and whom we fondly hope is stronger than the gods of other men? Ernest Fremont Tittle once suggested that many people "think of God, not only as a magnified man, but as a magnified white man, and more particularly still, as a magnified Englishman, who came to America in the May-flower, and, as quickly as possible, moved to Boston, where he has been living in cultivated seclusion ever since."[1]

Small wonder that we quake when crises come and fear that our god has forgotten us. He has, because he exists only in our own imagination. When this happens our god is too small. We need to rise to a rugged faith in the everlasting God, the rock from which we and all peoples were hewn (51:1). In him lies the path of peace; in common devotion to his ways is our only salvation.

We moderns no longer bow down to graven images, but idol worship is far from absent among us. An idol may be any idea or thing which commands our passionate or excessive devotion, especially if it is the work of our own hands or minds.

[1] *The Religion of the Spirit* (New York: Abingdon Press, 1928), p. 324. Used by permission of John M. Tittle.

For multitudes the chief object of trust, the main ground of hope, is money, success, prestige, popularity, power, military strength, technology, or the like—all unworthy substitutes for the most high God, and all alike incapable of yielding true satisfaction. Why do we "keep on praying to a god that cannot save"? (45:20) When real food is free,

> Why do you spend your money for that which
>   is not bread,
>   and your labor for that which does not satisfy?

> . . . .

> Incline your ear, and come to me;
>   hear, that your soul may live (55:1-3).

One evening in December 1955, a few days before Christmas, I lay in a hospital recuperating from a major operation, my second in six months. The night before, talented singers from the Harvard-Radcliffe Choral Society had gone through the halls cheering the patients with their beautiful carols. This evening there were no visible singers. But as I lay there alone in my discomfort I began reading the fortieth chapter of Isaiah. Suddenly I was not alone, but surrounded by angelic voices. Outside the temperature had dropped to zero, and the heating system was working overtime. In my radiator the steam throbbed rhythmically, while across the hall, as I later learned, water boiled noisily in the sterlizer. Yet what I heard was nothing so prosaic as steam or water, but celestial music.

Christmas carols filled the air—or rather a composition which was no one carol but all carols.

In sublime harmonies akin to a Bach chorale the voices were singing the words I was reading: "Do you say, 'My way is hid from the Lord?' . . . Have you not heard? . . . The Lord is the everlasting God, the Creator of the ends of the earth. He does not faint or grow weary . . . . He gives power to the faint, and to him who has no might he increases strength . . . . They who wait for the Lord shall renew their strength."

I was lifted as on eagle wings into the very presence of God. My weariness was gone. I knew that in his power and love I would be ready for whatever might be in store for me, whether joy or pain, whether running in some noteworthy service or walking in routine tasks. The assurance has remained, even though a year later another operation proved necessary. God's grace has exceeded my need.

To such a God, and to him alone, we are called to yield our lives in trustful obedience.

IX

YOUR GOD REIGNS

THE LORD OF HISTORY

NATURE AND HUMAN EVENTS: THE God of creation is also the Lord of history. Indeed, Seccnd Isaiah draws no sharp distinction between nature and human events. By his creative deed God brings into existence both the physical world and human society, and they continue under his sovereignty. Nature is the background for history, and history in turn provides the arena in which the purpose of creation is fulfilled.

God stretches out the heavens "like a tent *to dwell in*"; he who "sits above the circle of the earth" also controls the destinies of "the rulers of the earth" (40:22-23; see 42:5). The prophet asks the same kind of question regarding both activities: "Who has measured the waters? . . . Whom did he consult? . . . To whom then will you compare me? . . . Who stirred up one from the east? . . . Who has performed and done this, calling the generations from the beginning?" (40:12-14, 25; 41:2, 4, 26). The answer is always the same:

> I, the LORD, the first,
> and with the last; I am He (41:4).

The same Lord who forms light and darkness creates weal and woe in human life. His skies not only water the earth, but "rain down righteousness." "I am the Lord, who do all these things" (45:7-8).

The creation of the world and the deliverance of Israel from Egyptian bondage are the work of one God. Referring to an ancient Babylonian myth in which Marduk forms the heaven and earth by cutting Rahab the dragon in two, the poet asks,

> Was it not thou that didst cut Rahab in pieces,
> that didst pierce the dragon?
> Was it not thou that didst dry up the sea,
> the waters of the great deep;
> that didst make the depths of the sea a way
> for the redeemed to pass over? (51:9-10).

THE DIVINE ACTIVITY IN HISTORY: As Martin Buber has said, Second Isaiah is "the originator of a theology of world-history."[1] No thinker before him had ever attempted to understand the scattered occurrences of history in the light of a single principle, much less to see them as episodes in a divine drama. Isaiah had made a strong beginning in this direction, but it remained for his gifted successor to apply to the whole world and to all time what Isaiah had seen regarding a few nations and a brief period.

In spite of the arrogant pretensions of human rulers, before the Lord "the nations are like a drop from a bucket." They "are accounted as the

[1] *The Prophetic Faith*, p. 208.

dust on the scales," "as less than nothing and emptiness." He "brings princes to nought, and makes the rulers of the earth as nothing" (40:15, 17, 23). Ultimately it is his ends rather than theirs that are fulfilled (55:11). History is the sphere not of caprice but order and purpose. It is guided by the infinite wisdom and matchless power of God.

In history God is no mere spectator; his role is rather that of acting, participating, purposing, and fulfilling. Note the prominence of active verbs in this typical passage:

I am God, and there is none like me,
declaring the end from the beginning
and from ancient times things not yet *done*,
saying, "My counsel shall *stand*,
and I will *accomplish* all my purpose,"
calling a bird of prey from the east,
the man of my counsel from a far country.
I have *spoken*, and I will *bring* it *to pass*;
I have *purposed*, and I will *do* it (46:9-11).

In this context we can better understand the prophet's assertion (see pages 99-100) that the Lord alone can foretell future events. Divine knowledge and power go together. As everlasting sovereign, "the first and the last," God rules the entire course of human history. He therefore knows and controls the "outcome" as well as "the former things," the end as well as the beginning (40:28; 41:22; 44:6).

GOD AND THE COVENANT PEOPLE: The outstanding instance of the divine activity in history is found of course in the Jewish people. In response to God's call or election, Israel has entered into a covenant relation with him. As the bearer of a special revelation, she has a unique mission among the nations. God addresses her as

> You, Israel, my servant,
>> Jacob, whom I have chosen,
>> the offspring of Abraham, my friend;
> you whom I took from the ends of the earth,
>> and called from its farthest corners
>>> (41:8-9).

When the chosen servant fails to fulfill his mission, he falls under judgment. Israel has turned out to be blind and deaf (42:20). The people would not walk in the Lord's ways, which they knew, nor obey his laws, which he had revealed. This is why they were "robbed and plundered," "trapped in holes and hidden in prisons." Their national humiliation was less the triumph of their enemies than it was the discipline of the Lord (42:21-25).

But he who calls and chastens Israel will also deliver her. Even in her blindness she is still his "servant," and in her deafness she remains "my messenger," "my dedicated one" (42:19). Punishment for sin will not be her lot indefinitely. The Lord will accomplish his purposes through a restored Israel (44:24-26). She has drunk from his hand the cup of his wrath, and "to the dregs the bowl of staggering." Now forgiveness and comfort are hers (51:17, 22-23).

THE COMING DOWNFALL OF BABYLON: It is time for Babylon to reap the fruit of her pride, her lust for wealth and pleasure, and her ruthless conquest. The Lord will "perform his purpose" on her

(48:14). In a vivid taunt song (chapter 47), the poet pictures her shame. No longer the mistress of kingdoms, she whose campaigns produced so many widows will herself know widowhood and loss of children. Neither the sorceries of her magicians nor the divinations of her astrologers can ward off the disaster which is about to engulf her. The flame which she confronts is "no coal for warming oneself," "no fire to sit before!" It will consume, and no one can save her (47:14-15).

Both the downfall of Babylon and the redemption of Israel will be accomplished by "the Lord of hosts." He will work, however, through a human agent, Cyrus, "his anointed." The Persian advance confirmed the suspicions of many Jews that their God was impotent. On the contrary, declares the prophet, the overthrow of Babylon will demonstrate both the might and the mercy of God, for it will be used by him to effect the deliverance of Israel.

CYRUS, AGENT OF THE LORD: Addressing the "coastlands" (the eastern Mediterranean peoples) in the dramatic poem describing the trial of the nations, the poet asks,

> Who stirred up one from the east
> whom victory meets at every step?

The answer is "I, the Lord" (41:2, 25; 46:11). Addressing Israel, the prophet asserts that Cyrus is the Lord's "shepherd," and that he will fulfill the divine purpose, which includes the rebuilding of Jerusalem and the temple (44:23; 48:14-15).

The victories of Cyrus are not really his own accomplishments. It is the Lord who opens the way before him and crowns his efforts with success, even though Cyrus himself is not aware of this (45:1-6). Two purposes are served: the deliverance of "Israel my chosen," and the disclosure to all nations of the one true God.

I gird you, though you do not know me,
that men may know, from the rising of the sun
and from the west, that there is none
besides me.

Yet Cyrus was no mere puppet. As Sennacherib advanced the divine purposes while seeking his own (10:7), so Cyrus, who released rather than punished Judah, sought to serve not God but Marduk. He was probably motivated far less by the humanitarian desire to free the Jews than by the political aim of setting up in Palestine a buffer state between Egypt and himself. Yet somehow his free pursuit of his own ends was used by God to accomplish the divine aims. Cyrus thus became the agent of the Lord, not because his acts were rigidly determined, but because his human will was somehow overshadowed by the infinitely more powerful and righteous will of God. His actions thus became vehicles for the attainment of God's goals as well as his own.

GOD AND MODERN HISTORY

As an interpreter of history, Second Isaiah has at least three things to say to our contemporary world in its time of sorrows.

110

1. *God rules in history as judge.* The successive downfalls of Israel, Assyria, Babylon, Persia, Greece, and Rome, and, in modern times, of dictators like Napoleon and Hitler, are evidence of a moral structure in the universe that cannot be escaped. God's laws may not be broken with impunity; instead, we break ourselves upon them.

In World War I, and in the vindictive treaty that followed, we sowed the dragon's teeth which bore their horrible fruit in World War II. In World War II, and in the bitter struggle for power —territorial, economic, political, military, atomic, psychological—that succeeded it, we have come perilously close to losing all power over our own destinies, splitting the world into two hostile camps, and rushing headlong toward the possible destruction of civilized life on this planet.

In quest of security, East and West are engaged in a bitter arms race. As a result, at this writing, the Soviet Union cannot repay the loans of its citizens, who suffer acute shortages of ordinary consumer goods. In the United States millions feel the pinch of the heavy taxation needed for unprecedented peacetime military budgets, while adequate appropriations for the education of our children are denied. Yet in spite of this heavy price paid for security, insecurity grows in both lands.

In the Middle East the struggle for oil, pursued by foreign interests with scant regard for native populations or the welfare of humanity as a whole, has contributed to a series of economic and military crises which have threatened the peace of the world and made the oil itself more inaccessible.

Men are called to a life of sonship with God and cooperation with each other in trustful obedience to him. When they ignore him and seek purely human ends, they are bound inescapably toward chaos and frustration. The true nature of life, says Paul Scherer, may be pictured as a triangle, with God as the base and ourselves and others as the other two sides. Often we try to upend the triangle to make it rest on the human individual or human society as its foundation.[1] But this will not work. Life is stable and meaningful only when it is founded on God, and when persons and groups are united in him.

2. *God is acting positively in history to fulfill his purposes.* History is not a meaningless circular process; God is guiding it toward an end, working creatively and redemptively even when all outward signs point to the contrary. So subtle is his wisdom and so vast his power that he is able to use even evil, self-seeking men and movements in the attainment of his goals.

As the conquests of Babylon served to chasten Israel and those of Cyrus were instrumental in her deliverance, so many other events, originally indifferent to or opposed to the will of God, are yet made to serve that will. The crucifixion of Jesus seemed to crush all his hopes, but it proved the beginning of the mightiest movement in human history. His murderers became unwitting instru-

[1] Paul Scherer, *Event in Eternity*, pp. 56-57.

ments in spreading the teaching which they sought to suppress. The overthrow of Rome by barbarian hordes seemed an unmitigated evil, yet it introduced the invaders to Roman institutions and the Christian faith, thereby paving the way for the richer civilization of modern Europe. There are signs that even the staggering carnage of World War II and the threat of the H-bomb are being used by God to awaken men to their folly and sin. There is growing recognition that unlimited national sovereignty must be replaced by world community, that fundamental human rights must be extended to all peoples, that discriminations based on race, color, and national origin must end. The crises of late 1956 in Hungary and the Middle East aroused the United Nations to rapid and decisive action, revealing a hitherto undreamed of moral strength.

These events were not planned or set in motion by God, but by men pursuing their own selfish ends. Yet repeatedly God has been able to redirect the human energies thus released to advance his larger goals. As William James suggested, God often acts like a master chess player, who, without coercing his opponents, knows all their possible moves and uses those very moves to gain his victory.

3. *The future—our future—is in God's hands.* Even if men blow up the earth or render it uninhabitable, God will not be defeated He was before history and will continue his creative and redemptive work beyond history, fulfilling his

purposes in some other realm. Sustained by God, we need not quake in fear, but may look ahead in trust. In a profound sense history is *his story*, but his story is greater and longer than history. In this perspective we may sing, with Katharina von Schlegel:

> Be still, my soul: thy God doth undertake
>> To guide the future as He has the past,
> Thy hope, thy confidence let nothing shake;
>> All now mysterious shall be bright at last.[1]

In one of his most moving passages the poet writes,

> How beautiful upon the mountains
>> are the feet of him who brings good tidings,
> who publishes peace, who brings good
>> tidings of good,
>> who publishes salvation,
>> who says to Zion, "Your God reigns"
>> (Isa. 52:7).

More than 600 years later an inspired Christian, writing amid the dark days of Roman persecution, echoed the same exultant hope as he cried, "Hallelujah! For the Lord our God the Almighty reigns" (Rev. 19:6). Of his kingdom there shall be no end.

[1] *The Methodist Hymnal*, No. 73. Translated by Jane L. Borthwick.

114

X

SALVATION
TO THE END OF THE EARTH

For Second Isaiah, God is not only the sole Creator of the world and the Ruler of all human history. He is also the mighty Redeemer. He acts to renew and transform those whose sin has called forth judgment. His chastening is rooted in love and designed to produce the repentance which can receive forgiveness and lead to reconciliation. These poems breathe a spirit of tender compassion which places them, along with Hosea, closer to the heart of the Christian gospel than anything else in the Old Testament.

Just as there is for the poet no boundary between creation and history, so there is none between these and redemption. The three are parts of one divine drama. All creation and all history point toward the salvation which crowns and consummates the mighty acts of God. The prophet's use of the very word *create* makes plain this unity. God creates not only physical nature, but Israel (43:1, 7, 15), and "new things" in history (48:

6-7). He even creates salvation and righteousness. (45:8). The same "arm of the Lord" which created the universe and brought Israel, "the redeemed," through the Red Sea will enable "the ransomed of the Lord" to return "and come with singing to Zion" (51:9-11). Extended through Israel to all peoples, this redemption fulfills both creation and the history which binds together beginning and end.

THE MEANING OF SALVATION

Words like redemption and salvation arouse little interest among many persons today. We easily dismiss them as over-pious and other-worldly, inappropriate for flesh-and-blood people with a healthy interest in the here and now. Doubtless there is something wholesome in such a view. Few can sing, "Jerusalem the golden, would God I were in thee," and really mean it. And many who speak most glibly of their own salvation are guilty of an insufferable holier-than-thou attitude or of evading their responsibilities toward their fellow men.

But which of us does not need to be saved now from fear, anxiety, and guilt, and lifted to hope, faith, and forgiveness? And who can stifle the question of his own relation to eternity? Furthermore, what is more practical than to ask how our world can be saved from self-destruction and become a just and peaceful human family? Salvation is a great and relevant word, and Second Isaiah can enrich its meaning for both present and future.

Six times he uses the Hebrew word translated *deliverance*, and four times the verb *deliver*. The term *salvation* itself appears ten times, while the noun *Savior* and the verb *save* appear three times each. On twelve occasions the poet refers to God as *Redeemer*, and eighteen times he uses the verb *redeem*. The reality to which such terms refer is a constantly recurring theme of the poems.

The concreteness of the Hebrew notion of salvation is clear from the Arabic root[1] of the word, which means "room"; literally, to be saved means to have room to move around in freely. The term would have peculiar meaning for captives who for decades have been confined to a narrow territory, and for whom freedom of movement is only a memory and a dream. With similar import, Christians call Savior one who came that men might have life, and life more abundantly.

The word *redeemer* is derived from ancient family law. When, for example, a person had been sold into slavery, his nearest male kinsman was expected to buy his freedom and thus restore the family solidarity. This relative was the redeemer. In the context of the intimate covenant relation between God and Israel, the term was readily broadened and applied to God, who assumed responsibility for freeing his enslaved people.

The redemption promised by Second Isaiah is both outward and inward. *Externally*, it involves release from bondage, judgment on Israel's oppressors, a return to Palestine, the restoration of

---

[1] Arabic, *wesha*; Hebrew, *yesha*.

Jerusalem, the temple, and the land, and the conversion of other peoples to Israel's religion. *Spiritually*, it means forgiveness, reconciliation with God, and divine strengthening for a new life.

The salvation of God is extended to other peoples as well as Israel. Second Isaiah is thus in the fullest sense the prophet of universalism. Initially, God acts to redeem the Jews, but they in turn are called to be "a light to the nations." "Every one who thirsts," whatever his nationality, is invited to partake of the wine and milk which cannot be bought but are gifts from God (55:1).

THE REDEEMER OF ISRAEL

In a variety of ways Second Isaiah makes plain the special place held by Israel in God's redemptive activity. For him as for Isaiah the Lord is typically "the Holy One of Israel." Just as frequently he is "the Redeemer." Often the two are combined; in such instances the Lord is described more intimately as "your Savior" or "our Redeemer" (43:3; 47:4).

The intimacy of the relation appears particularly in the terms applied to Israel. She is "my servant," "my chosen," "my nation," "my people" (42:1-2; 51:4, 16; 44:1-2). The Lord of hosts is her husband; he has called her "like a wife forsaken and grieved in spirit" (54:5-6; 51:1-2). Conceivably a mother might forget the infant she has nursed or refuse mercy to her son, but God will not forget Israel (49:15). She sinned grievously, so that in

118

anger the Lord hid his face "for a moment." However, she is not finally cast off, but forgiven. Her transgressions are blotted out, swept away like a cloud of mist (43:25; 44:22; 54:7-8).

"For the mountains may depart
and the hills be removed,
but my steadfast love shall not depart from you,
and my covenant of peace shall not be
removed" (54:10).

Hence the Redeemer "comes" and leads his exiles home. He assures them that his strength will equip them for the trials of the journey, leveling the mountains and valleys and smoothing out the rough places (40:3-4). They need not go in haste, as though in flight. The Lord himself will go before them and also be their "rear guard" (52:12).

"Fear not, for I am with you,
be not dismayed, for I am your God;
I will strengthen you, I will help you,
I will uphold you with my victorious right
hand" (41:10).

No danger will be too great to be endured.

"Fear not, for I have redeemed you;
I have called you by name, you are mine.
When you pass through the waters I will be
with you;
and through the rivers, they shall not
overwhelm you;
when you walk through fire you shall not be
burned,
and the flame shall not consume you"
(43:1-2).

There is a double imagery in this journey to freedom. God guides his people from Babylon back to Palestine, even as, centuries before, he led them through the wilderness from Egypt to Canaan. But both events have a deeper meaning. The wilderness wanderings led to Sinai and a sacred covenant, and thence to the promised land. So now the divinely-led return to the land heralds the new age which will fulfill God's purpose in the covenant, accomplishing the end which he has cherished for Israel. "Behold, the Lord God comes with might" (40:10). How appropriate that nature itself should awaken to new life, sing with joy, and glorify God! (41:17-20; 51:3; 55:12-13)

A LIGHT TO THE NATIONS

ISRAEL'S MISSION TO THE WORLD: Great as is God's love for Israel, it reaches out to include the whole world. Hence the Hebrew people are not chosen for special privilege or authority, but for service. God's action to redeem them is but a stage in his work of redeeming all peoples. Part of the purpose of the covenant itself was that Israel might be "a light to the nations" (42:6). As the servant of the Lord, she is chosen to establish justice among the peoples and to spread salvation (42:4; 49:1-6; 52:10). When "the glory of the Lord" is revealed, "all flesh shall see it together" (40:5).

> "It is too light a thing that you should be
>   my servant
>   to raise up the tribes of Jacob
>   and to restore the preserved of Israel;
> I will give you as a light to the nations,
>   that my salvation may reach to the end of
>   the earth" (49:6).

The invitation is therefore universal:

> "Turn to me and be saved,
>> all the ends of the earth!
>> For I am God, and there is no other.
> By myself I have sworn,
>> from my mouth has gone forth in righteousness
>> a word that shall not return
> 'To me every knee shall bow,
>> every tongue shall swear' " (45:22-23).

GOD'S NEW ERA: The result of the redemptive action of God will be the end of the present age and the establishment of God's new era. Unlike any created thing—even the heavens and the earth which seem to men so enduring—the Lord's salvation is everlasting. It is as eternal as it is universal. Even now it is about to be ushered in by his victorious power:

> "My deliverance draws near speedily,
>> my salvation has gone forth,
>> and my arms will rule the peoples;
> the coastlands wait for me,
>> and for my arm they hope.
> Lift up your eyes to the heavens,
>> and look at the earth beneath;
> for the heavens will vanish like smoke,
>> the earth will wear out like a garment,
>> and they who dwell in it will die like gnats;
> but my salvation will be forever,
>> and my deliverance will never be ended"
>> (51:5-6).

Carried away by the expectation of so momentous an event, the poet summons all men to lift their voices in exultation:

Sing to the Lord a new song,
   his praise from the end of the earth!
   (42:10).

THE TRANSFORMATION OF NATURE: So all-encompassing is to be the coming redemption that the prophet portrays it as involving even the transformation of nature. Possibly his language is meant to be taken quite realistically, since he knows no clear separation between physical and spiritual. But whether we interpret him literally or figuratively, his lines speak eloquently of the limitless scope of God's saving activity.

In one vivid passage the renewal of nature expresses the Lord's concern for Israel. Water will spring forth in the dry land and trees will flourish in what was formerly desert, that men may know that the hand of the Lord, the Holy One of Israel, has done it (41:18-20).

However, in the closing lines of the poem the transformation of the physical world typifies the universality of God's salvation:

"For you shall go out in joy,
   and be led forth in peace;
the mountains and the hills before you
   shall break forth into singing,
      and all the trees of the field shall clap
         their hands.
Instead of the thorn shall come up the cypress;
   instead of the brier shall come up the myrtle;
and it shall be to the Lord for a memorial,
   for an everlasting sign which shall not be
      cut off" (55:12-13).

Christians today, even more than the peoples of 540 B. C., are called to "sing to the Lord a new song." What was then still a hope has become for us a glorious reality. Second Isaiah's song of redemption, raised to a higher key in Jesus Christ. has two great themes for the Church of our time.

1. We, too, may be delivered by divine grace from the power of sin to a life of righteousness in fellowship with him. God has acted and is acting to give us victory over those ways of thought and life which separate us from him and from each other. He offers us his forgiving and transforming love. When we turn to him in repentance, trust, and obedience, we experience the restoration of inner harmony, the re-establishment of right human relations, and reconciliation with God. This is salvation.

2. We, too, are called to be "a light to the nations." God's redemptive love knows no boundaries, but embraces the entire world. In the words of the Negro spiritual, "He's got the whole world in his hand." Those who have received from him the gift of newness of life are commissioned to share it with all mankind.

The Jews as a nation never fully grasped or accepted their vocation. The temptation to keep the good news to themselves proved too great. But there is even less excuse for the Christian Church to mistake mission for special favor. What we have freely received we must freely give, *else we ourselves shall lose it.* The new life dies unless it is shared. Even more than ancient Israel, the Church is summoned to be the *agent* as well as the *recipient* of God's salvation.

Ruth Seabury tells a moving story of Marcolino, a chieftain's son in Portuguese West Africa, who became a missionary along the frontier of his country. With four of his laymen he journeyed three days by bicycle to Angola to meet her and discuss his Christian faith and task. As they parted, one of the group said with deep insight, "You are going out through the door that you have opened for us, a big, wide door to the world. We are never going to let it get shut! Now we know that when you join the Church of Christ, *you join a world thing.*"[1] By the grace of God we Christians do belong to "a world thing." To people all over the world we are called to open doors from darkness into light, from fear into hope, from death into life.

Second Isaiah is the Old Testament's noblest exponent of the missionary spirit. He is speaking directly to us. We too are called to be bearers of the wondrous news, witnesses to the divine love which alone can redeem the world.

> Get you up to a high mountain,
> O Zion, herald of good tidings;
>
> . . . .
>
> say to the cities of [all the earth],
> "Behold your God!" (40:9)

[1] Ruth Isabel Seabury, *So Send I You* (Philadelphia: Christian Education Press, 1955), pp. 108-9. Used by permission.

XI

WITH HIS STRIPES
WE ARE HEALED

"**B**EHOLD my servant, whom I uphold" (42:1).
Between these words and those which close our
preceding chapter there is much more than a verbal
connection. The activity of God is seen most truly
in the life of his "servant," who is presented with
cumulative power in four songs which gather up
the deepest meanings of the prophet's message
(42:1-4; 49:1-6; 50:4-9; 52:13 through 53:12).[1]

These four songs differ significantly from the
other poems which mention a servant. They refer
to the servant as an individual, use a different
rhythm, and at some points employ a distinctive
vocabulary. Such features not only serve to identify
the songs, but raise some doubt as to whether they
and the other poems are the work of the same
author.

On the whole, however, the language, style, and
literary form of the songs and the poems are strik-
ingly parallel; they deal repeatedly with similar

[1] Some students believe 42:5-7 (or 5-9), 49:7-9a, and 50:1-3 are
possibly secondary servant songs.

125

motifs; and their religious ideas are altogether harmonious. Moreover, the servant passages fit perfectly into the structure of the stanzas which precede and follow them, the first three belonging clearly to larger literary units. Most scholars therefore regard them as written by Second Isaiah himself, probably in the closing days of the exile.

THE IDENTITY OF THE SERVANT

Who is the servant? Many interpreters identify him with some historical individual, such as Jeremiah, Cyrus, or Nehemiah; others, with the figure of the coming Messiah. Still others uphold a corporate interpretation, regarding the servant as Israel, ideal or actual, or as a faithful remnant or spiritual nucleus within the nation.

Convincing evidence for the collective view is the explicit statement in 49:3: "You are my servant, Israel, in whom I will be glorified." Numerous passages outside the servant songs make the same identification (see 41:8; 43:10; 44:1-2, 21; 45:4). Moreover, the Septuagint translation, in a sense the oldest interpretation of 42:1, inserts "Jacob" and "Israel" before "servant" and "chosen." If Second Isaiah is the author of the songs, it seems overwhelmingly probable that he identifies the servant with Israel throughout his book.

There are two main difficulties with this conclusion. First, the servant in the four songs is actually pictured as an individual person. The fourth in particular narrates the story of one who suffers and dies for others. However, an individual could hardly triumph apart from a resurrection, which is not mentioned; whereas Israel as a nation could quite understandably be spoken of as dying (when carried into captivity) and being glorified (after the exile). Moreover, the references to the servant in the songs are hardly more individualistic than elsewhere.

Secondly, in 49:5-6 the servant seems sharply distinguished from Israel, with a mission to Israel. He is called to "raise up the tribes of Jacob and to restore the preserved of Israel." However, the servant here may signify the true Israel within Israel, the faithful core which has not succumbed to pagan ways of life and worship. The members of this group have a mission to both their own nation and other peoples. They are to embody the spirit of sacrificial suffering for others by which Israel as a whole may in turn bring healing to the nations. Historically, Israel had fallen far short of manifesting this spirit. Yet in comparison with other nations she appeared to Second Isaiah as relatively righteous. He could thus visualize her, chastened by centuries of suffering and inspired by her most spiritually sensitive citizens, as chosen by the Lord to fulfill his purposes.

The prophet's picture of the servant fits no historical individual; on the other hand, it harmonizes well with the kind of community he conceives Israel to be capable of becoming. In a twofold sense, therefore, we may think of the servant of the Lord as a servant-community, a kind of corporate personality: he is the Israel that already exists in the inner nucleus of dedicated souls; and he is the larger Israel which God calls the whole nation to be.

THE CHARACTER AND MISSION
OF THE SERVANT

More important than the identity of the servant are his character and significance. There is a dramatic movement of thought from the first song, which contains no suggestion of the servant's martyrdom, to the fourth, which pictures his agonizing suffering resulting in death. This change may represent intentional construction, or it may reflect the author's deepening insight as God reveals to him the meaning of his people's sufferings.

INTRODUCTION OF THE SERVANT: In the first song (42:1-4) the Lord introduces the servant, whom he has appointed much as an earthly king names his chief official. The words of approval, "in whom my soul delights," are uttered also by the heavenly voice at Jesus' baptism and at his transfiguration (Mark 1:11; Matt. 17:5). Endowed with power from above, the servant will faithfully establish among the nations the righteousness ordained by God—a service emphasized by the three-fold repetition of the Hebrew *mishpat*, justice. Even so, he will work quietly without fanfare. The figures of the reed and the wick may reflect symbolic legal proceedings. In ancient Babylonia transfers of land were accompanied by the symbolic transmission of a wooden object resembling a reed. The lamp has long symbolized human rights.[1] The poet may mean that the servant will not destroy the land rights and personal freedoms which were for Jews in Babylon almost extinct, but rather renew and extend true freedom among all men.

THE CALL OF THE SERVANT: In the second song (Isa. 49:1-6) the servant himself addresses the nations, first describing his divine call and equipment. Since he is to utter the word of God, his mouth receives special attention. So powerful is the divine message that it is pictured as a sharp sword and a polished arrow, while the Lord protects his servant until the appointed time by hiding him in a quiver. Israel's task is to glorify God. But as he looks back on his labors, like Isaiah and Jeremiah, the servant is conscious of failure. Men have not listened. Nevertheless, he leaves the results of his work to God, in whose presence he finds his strength and reward. The poem becomes more intelligible if, following the suggestion of James Muilenburg, we place the last two lines of verse five immediately after verse four, the thought of which they complete.[2]

In verse five the servant seems to be called "to bring Jacob back," which he can hardly do if he is identical with the nation. However, the difficulty is removed if we think of the servant as the faithful community within Israel. In the closing verse the servant is reminded that it is not enough for his

[1] J. Begrich, *Studien zu Deutero-jesaja* (W. Kohlhammer: Stuttgart, 1936) , pp. 136,163-164.
[2] Exegesis of Isaiah 40-66, *The Interpreter's Bible*, V, 564, 568.

own people to be redeemed. In addition to being an end in itself, the restoration of Israel is also a means to the salvation of the world. In spite of his sense of failure, the servant is therefore given a still greater task, that of being "a light to the nations."

THE SERVANT UPHELD BY GOD: In the third song (50:4-9), the word translated "those who are taught" is the same *limmudim* which occurs in 8:16, and nowhere else in the Old Testament. This suggests the possibility that Second Isaiah belonged to a prophetic group spiritually descended from the band of disciples formed by Isaiah almost two centuries earlier. (See pp. 51-52.) The servant-disciple is given the capacity to hear as well as to proclaim the Lord's message. Throughout the biblical writings the ear is the chief organ through which men receive the revelation of God. The servant listens attentively, responds obediently, and utters the divine word which upholds the weary.

As he carries out his mission he arouses severe persecution. The smiters and beard-pullers may refer to those Jews who resented the extension to other peoples of the salvation which they felt belonged exclusively to Israel. The stringency of the opposition is indicated by the legal terms employed to describe it: vindicate, contend, stand up, adversary, guilty. But the servant faces his enemies unflinchingly. He can endure whatever comes in the strength of the God who is with him and in the assurance that God's cause will triumph: "He who vindicates me is near."

THE SUFFERING AND VICTORY OF THE SERVANT:
The fourth song (52:13 through 53:12) has been
extolled as "the most influential poem in any
literature."[1] Its portrayal of the role of the servant
provided the basis for Jesus' conception of his
own mission, as well as for the explanation of his
death which became central in the evangel of the
Christian Church. Its disclosure of *the redemptive
power of unmerited suffering borne for others* has
brought comfort to uncounted multitudes and
imparted meaning to their sorrow. So powerful
and dramatic is the poem and so sensitively does
it plumb the depths of reality that no interpretation
can do justice to it.

Of the five three-verse stanzas, the first and
last present the words of the Lord, while the intervening three voice the confession of the nations, possibly in the words of their kings. Relating the history of Israel to that of the nations,
the poem contrasts the humiliation and exaltation,
the suffering and victory of the servant, with the
emphasis as a whole on triumph through suffering.

In the opening stanza God introduces the servant as one horribly disfigured by the unjustified
hardships he has endured. A dread disease like
leprosy would fit the description well. Before such
a spectacle the other nations are astounded, and
when their kings understand the cause they are
moved to silent awe. Yet the ultimate outcome will
be the exaltation of the servant.

[1] Henry Sloane Coffin, Exposition of Isaiah 40-66, *The Interpreter's
Bible* V, 614.

The next three stanzas express the lamenting response of the kings. What they have heard seems unbelievable, yet they are forced to confess its truth. How dismal was the external history of Israel! The people had emerged from slavery in Egypt only to wander for years in the wilderness, then required almost two centuries to occupy a narrow strip of land in Palestine. After scarcely a century of relative prosperity, the nation was torn asunder by rebellion. Both resultant kingdoms endured many years of foreign oppression, and both finally succumbed to invasion and were carried into captivity. Such a people could command no respect among the great and powerful; inevitably it "was despised and rejected by men."

As the speakers painfully realize that they have shared the common attitude toward the servant—"we esteemed him not"—they receive a breathtaking insight. Somehow his sufferings have been *for them*. He has borne the consequences not of his own sin but of theirs, and for their sake. Moved by this consciousness to confess their iniquity, they are forgiven and made whole. Behind the whole series of events is the redemptive will of God, who uses the anguish of his servant to reconcile the nations to himself:

> He was wounded for our transgressions,
> he was bruised for our iniquities;
> upon him was the chastisement that made us whole,
> and with his stripes we are healed (53:5).

All this the servant has endured willingly, and in love. Like a lamb being sacrificed or a sheep being sheared, he has not protested. Verse eight is somewhat obscure, but with verse nine may perhaps be paraphrased: Following imprisonment and an unjust sentence, the servant was led away to death. He suffered for the sins of others, but none of his contemporaries understood. In death, as in life, he was associated with evil-doers—"a rich man" is here probably synonymous with "the wicked"—though he was guiltless in both word and deed.

In an impassioned climax (53:10-12), God again speaks, at first in the third person. Here three notes previously struck blend in a chord of profound beauty: (1) The whole career of the faithful servant actually fulfills the saving purpose of God. (2) By taking voluntarily on himself the consequences of the sins of others, he becomes the means whereby they are treated as righteous and restored to God. Even while facing death he intercedes for those whose sin has caused his death [1] (3) The servant will be rewarded with descendants, long life, and great power. "He shall prolong his days" (53:10) probably signifies the resurrection of the servant, that is, the restoration of Israel after exile.[2] The song ends as it begins, with the promised exaltation of him who gives himself vicariously for the sake of others.

[1] Note the similarity of verse 12 to Jesus' prayer from the cross: "Father, forgive them; for they know not what they do" (Luke 23:34).
[2] Since belief in the resurrection of the individual arose in Hebrew thought much later than the sixth century B.C., this verse clearly points to the community of Israel as the servant.

THE SERVANT AND JESUS CHRIST

Rather than a prediction, the servant songs are an inspired portrayal of the true meaning of the history of the covenant people. Further, they are a summons to Israel to accept and carry out her high mission as the suffering servant of the Lord, thereby bringing redemption to the nations. The call was never heeded, either by Israel as a whole or by a faithful minority.

Nevertheless, the songs were in the deepest sense prophetic. Almost six centuries later, they found fulfillment in an individual. Christians have rightly seen in the life, passion, death, and resurrection of Jesus Christ, the Redeemer through whose sufferings men are reconciled to God. Jesus apparently thought of himself as the suffering servant. The New Testament writers repeatedly make the same identification, finding particularly in Isaiah 53 the clue to the meaning of Jesus' suffering, death, and victory.[1] From the beginning the gospel proclaimed by the Christian Church has centered in the story of one who was wounded for our transgressions. It was thus given to Second Isaiah to foreshadow in his servant poems the deepest meaning of the Christian revelation. For centuries unaccepted and only dimly grasped, his

[1] The following typical passages, with the relevant servant passages from Isaiah, listed in parentheses, are worth careful study by all Christians who seek deeper spiritual understanding: Matt. 3:17 (42:1) ; 12:18-21 (42:1-4) ; 17:5 (42:1) ; Mark 9:12 (53) ; 10:45 (53) ; 14:24 (53:12) ; Luke 22:37 (53:12) ; Acts 3:13, 26; 4:27, 30 (42:1; 49:3; 52:13); Acts 8:30-35 and I Cor. 15:3 (53:5-12); Heb. 9:28 (53:11-12); I Peter 1:19 (53:7); 2:22-25 (53:5-6, 9, 12); Rev. 5:6-14 (53:7).

sublime insights were finally in Jesus Christ translated from idea to historic reality.

This compels the followers of Christ to ask some searching questions. Does not the life of the Lord's Servant offer guidance for worshipers of the Servant's Lord? The suffering love extolled by Second Isaiah and incarnated in Jesus is asserted by Christians to be the greatest power in the world. Why do we revere it in Jesus and practice it so feebly ourselves? We declare that God himself works redemptively through those who suffer willingly for the sake of others. Why then do we guard so zealously our own comfort and think first of our own security? We know the Church is called to carry on the reconciling work begun by Christ. Why are we so often indifferent to our mission, joining instead the ranks of those who need to be reconciled?

The choice is ours. We may, like ancient Israel, reject our call. Or we may, as faithful servants of God, take on ourselves the burdens and pain of the world in that self-forgetful love which makes men whole.

Part Four

ISAIAH, CHAPTERS 56-66

XII

TO REVIVE THE HEART
OF THE CONTRITE

THE BACKGROUND OF ISAIAH 56
THROUGH 66

Differences in content, implied setting, emphasis, and tone indicate, as noted on page 84, that the closing chapters of Isaiah were written at a later date than chapters 40 through 55, and by a different author. The situation is apparently that of Palestine after the return of the exiles in 537 B.C., but before the rebuilding of the walls of Jerusalem under Nehemiah in 445 B.C. Some passages assume that the rebuilding of the temple (520-516 B.C.) has already occurred, while others imply the opposite. Various specific dates have been suggested and supported, but none can claim certainty. The most we can say with definiteness is that chapters 56 through 66 were written some time during the century following the Babylonian Exile.

In spite of the differences mentioned, chapters 56 through 66 do manifest real similarities to 40 through 55 in thought, language, and style. The later poems reveal the strong influence of the earlier ones, and represent the same prophetic tradition. Probably they are the work of a disciple or disciples of Second Isaiah. The inner divergences may be due to multiple authorship, or they may be ascribed to changing moods and emphases of one writer, who is often called Third Isaiah.

These chapters are in the main an adaptation of the ideas of Second Isaiah to changed circumstances. The decades following the return of the exiles were marked by disillusionment. The high hopes aroused by their deliverance remained unfulfilled. The situation was new, but it bore little resemblance to the new age anticipated by the devout. The purposes of God had not been consummated. Material poverty prevailed, and the Lord had not redeemed his people. Gentiles had not turned in large numbers to the God of Israel. Some indeed had come, but with them came alien religious practices and their corrupting influences. Ritualistic observances were frequently unaccompanied by true reverence or lives ethically devoted to God. Many of the faithful asked: "Why does the Lord postpone his coming?" Others were baffled by the practical problems of reconstruction. The result was a people disappointed and discouraged. The prophecies of Isaiah 56 through 66 attempt to deal with this situation within the context of Second Isaiah's messages to an earlier generation.

THE MESSAGE

The main content of the poems is accurately suggested in the simple outline of Julius A. Bewer:[1] (1) problems of the returned community (56 through 58); (2) Zion's restoration and future glory (59:1 through 63:6); (3) penitential prayer for the renewal of God's love (63:7 through 64:12); (4) blessings for the faithful; punishment for the apostates (65 and 66).

Instead of the unity and dramatic progression so evident in Second Isaiah, these chapters are marked by contrast and alternation of thought. We can best understand the message of the poems and their meaning for our own lives if we examine a number of these contrasts. Some seem to represent genuine inconsistency. Others merely reflect alternating emphases or offer realistic interpretations of actual situations. In still others close scrutiny reveals different but not contradictory aspects of one underlying conviction.

1. WARNING AND HOPE: The prophecies voice both warning and hope, reproof and consolation. "The hand of the Lord is with his servants," but "his indignation is against his enemies" (66:14). On the one hand, the distress of the people is due to their own sin, not to God's failure to fulfill his promises. He was ready to be sought and found, but those whom he awaited did not seek him or call on his name. Instead, they followed their own devices (65:1-2), and cut themselves off from God.

[1] *The Book of Isaiah*, Harper's Annotated Bible (New York: Harper & Bros., 1950), Vol. 2, p. 51.

> Behold, the LORD's hand is not shortened,
> that it cannot save,
> or his ear dull, that it cannot hear;
> but your iniquities have made a separation
> between you and your God,
> and your sins have hid his face from you
> so that he does not hear (59:1-2).

Those who practice deceit and injustice accomplish their own destruction. Their rejection of God's righteous will brings inevitable retribution (59:18). "There is no peace . . . for the wicked" (57:21). The same fate confronts those who "forsake the Lord" to offer food and wine to "Fortune" and "Destiny."[1] They too are doomed (65:11-12).

On the other hand, those who come to God in obedient trust find in him their Redeemer (59:20).

> Before they call I will answer,
> while they are yet speaking I will hear
> (65:24).

"Prepare the way," cries the poet,
> "Say to the daughter of Zion,
> 'Behold, your salvation comes;
> behold, his reward is with him,
> and his recompense before him.'
> And they shall be called The holy people,
> The redeemed of the LORD" (62:10-12).

In one of the noblest of all poems, the prophet heralds the coming day of salvation (61). The opening lines are so similar in spirit to the servant passages that some scholars identify the speaker with the servant. It seems more likely that the prophet is voicing his own sense of call.

[1] The gods Bel and Meni.

142

The Spirit of the Lord GOD is upon me,
  because the LORD has anointed me
to bring good tidings to the afflicted;
  he has sent me to bind up the brokenhearted,
to proclaim liberty to the captives
  and the opening of the prison to
    those who are bound;
to proclaim the year of the LORD's favor,
  and the day of vengeance of our God
    (61:1-2).

So perfectly do these words express the meaning of the promised fulfillment that Jesus quotes them as he begins his sermon at Nazareth (Luke 4: 18-19). Significantly, he omits the line announcing vengeance. Indeed, Muilenburg and others believe *requital* or *rescue* would render better the basic meaning of the Hebrew word; such a translation would also accord with the whole tenor of the chapter.

The closing lines of the poem reach a climax reminiscent of Isaiah 55:10-11.

For as the earth brings forth its shoots,
  and as a garden causes what is sown in it
    to spring up,
so the Lord GOD will cause righteousness
  and praise
  to spring forth before all the nations
    (61:11).

Like his anonymous predecessor, Third Isaiah pictures the new age with metaphors drawn from nature. The Lord will "create new heavens and a new earth" (65:17; 66:22). The present world will be wholly transformed. Here as in Genesis and Second Isaiah, creation provides the setting for

143

history. God is sovereign over both and works in both to accomplish his salvation—a new creation.[1]

2. ALL ISRAEL OR THE REPENTANT? Some passages seem to expect all Israel to share in the coming redemption, while others include only the pious. On the one hand, the vindication of Zion will be so plain that the nations will see her in glory (62:1-2). Her people "shall all be righteous," and "shall possess the land forever," so that the Lord "may be glorified" (60:21). A new era is coming in which the sons and daughters of Israel will gather from afar.

> Arise, shine; for your light has come,
>   and the glory of the LORD has risen
>   upon you.
> For behold, darkness shall cover the earth,
>   and thick darkness the peoples;
> but the LORD will arise upon you,
>   and his glory will be seen upon you.
> And nations shall come to your light,
>   and kings to the brightness of your
>   rising (60:1-3; see verses 4-7).

Other passages emphatically exclude from this consummation the faithless workers of evil:

> "Behold, my servants shall eat,
>   but you shall be hungry;
> behold, my servants shall drink,
>   but you shall be thirsty;
> behold, my servants shall rejoice,
>   but you shall be put to shame;
> behold, my servants shall sing for gladness
>   of heart,

[1] For other passages voicing reproof and judgment, see Isaiah 57:20-21; 58:1-5; 66:3-6, 15-17. For additional expressions of hope and promise, see 57:15; 60:17-22; 62:3-4; 65:8-10.

> but you shall cry out for pain of heart,
> and shall wail for anguish of spirit:"
> > (65:13-14; see 57:20-21; 59:15-19;
> > 66:4-6).

Yet there is no real inconsistency between these varying expectations. Restoration to divine favor is not automatic, but conditioned on repentance.

> For thus says the high and lofty One
> > who inhabits eternity, whose name is Holy:
> "I dwell in the high and holy place,
> > and also with him who is of a contrite and
> > > humble spirit,
> to revive the spirit of the humble,
> > and to revive the heart of the contrite"
> > > (57:15; see 66:2).

In steadfast love, God seeks to draw men to himself; those who turn from sin he heals (57:18; 59:20-21), while those who refuse his grace he allows to go their way to destruction (59:17-18; 65:1-7). When, therefore, vindication and salvation are promised to Israel, it is reasonable to assume that repentant Israel alone is implied. The prophet need not always make this explicit.

3. NATIONALISM AND UNIVERSALISM: The attitude toward aliens combines considerable breadth with an assumption of Jewish supremacy. Foreigners and eunuchs "who join themselves to the Lord" are granted full religious fellowship, provided they keep the sabbath and the requirements of the Mosaic covenant. Such proselytes will be honored in the house of God. The joy of the temple worship will be theirs, and their prayers and sacrifices will be gladly accepted,

"for my house shall be called a house of prayer
   for all peoples" (56:3-8).[1]

The poems mount to a climax with a stirring re-
affirmation of religious universalism which suggests the exalted expectation of Second Isaiah:
"From new moon to new moon,
   and from sabbath to sabbath,
all flesh shall come to worship before me,"
   says the LORD (66:23; see 40:5).

However, though Third Isaiah recognizes true
community in worship, he does not extend it to
the rest of life. Foreigners are in fact assigned a
distinctly subordinate position. Jews are to be the
priests and ministers of God; they will in turn be
served by the aliens in their midst, even by kings.
The descendants of their oppressors will bow at
their feet. Foreigners shall rebuild their walls,
feed their flocks, and be their plowmen and vine-
dressers. The wealth of the nations will be brought
to Israel, and kingdoms that refuse subjection will
be laid waste. The precious woods of Lebanon—
cypress, plane, and pine—will be brought to
beautify the temple (60:10-14; 61:5-6).

Totally lacking is the call to Israel to lose herself as the Lord's servant in the redemption of
mankind. She is not servant but sovereign. The
roads connecting Israel and the nations are all
one-way streets. The inhabitants of Mount Zion
do not go out as missionaries to other peoples;
they do welcome citizens of other lands who come
to vow homage to the God of Israel. One suspects

[1] Jesus quotes this passage in driving the money-changers from the
temple (Mark 11:17 and parallels).

146

that even this welcome is extended partly because the acceptance of it will constitute an admission by the alien worshipers of Israel's supremacy.

4. RITUAL AND RIGHTEOUSNESS: The prophet lays great stress on purity of ritualistic and ceremonial observance, at the same time upholding ethical and spiritual religion in the noblest prophetic tradition. Some critics, in fact, censure him for failing to discriminate between ritual and moral offenses.

Those who keep the sabbath and the Mosaic law win the approval of God, and their sacrifices are acceptable to him (56:2-7; 58:13). On the other hand, those who eat "swine's flesh," "mice," and the "broth of abominable things"—sacrificial flesh forbidden as unclean in Levitical law—are a "smoke in my nostrils" (65:4-5; 66:17). Particularly condemned are those who have debased their worship with elements drawn from repulsive Canaanite cults: those "who burn with lust among the oaks," "who slay young children in the valleys," and who "have set your bed" on a high mountain (57:3-13; 66:3-4). Reference is obviously to the practice of human sacrifice, the sex cults, and the fertility rites which apparently have corrupted the worship of the Jews, though they still deceitfully pretend to worship the Lord. With disdainful irony the prophet invites such worshipers to seek deliverance at the hands of their alien gods. They will then discover that their true refuge lies in God alone (57:13).

Interwoven with this concern for acceptable

modes of worship is a profound insistence on right living. The Lord requires of his worshipers righteousness, justice, truth, and honesty (56:1; 61:8); on the contrary, injustice of all kinds, deeds of violence, deceit, and dishonesty separate men from him (59:1-15). Self-mortification is of no value if it is only an external form. Fasting which is accompanied by self-seeking, oppression of workers, quarreling, and fighting is repulsive to God. Merely sitting in sackcloth and ashes avails nothing. Rather,

> "Is not this the fast that I choose:
>   to loose the bonds of wickedness,
>   to undo the thongs of the yoke,
> to let the oppressed go free,
>   and to break every yoke?
> Is it not to share your bread with the hungry,
>   and bring the homeless poor into your house;
> when you see the naked, to cover him,
>   and not to hide yourself from your own
>   flesh?
> Then shall your light break forth like the dawn,
>   and your healing shall spring up speedily;
> your righteousness shall go before you,
>   the glory of the Lord shall be your rear
>   guard" (58:6-8; see verses 9-14).

Even the rebuilding of the temple will not satisfy God. Heaven is his throne and the earth is his footstool; what need has he of a man-built house? The dwelling he really seeks is in men who are "humble and contrite in spirit" (66:1-2).

The same attitude infuses the remarkable intercessory prayer of penitence (63:7 through 64:12) in which the prophet identifies himself with errant Israel. In deep agony he recounts the spiritual history of his people, confesses their sins, and pleads for forgiveness. The conception of God and his relation with Israel is one of the loftiest in the Old Testament. He is "our Father, our Redeemer from of old" who in "steadfast love" has fashioned Israel to be his holy people. He is the "holy Spirit" who has led them and in pity shares their afflictions. Significantly, the sin confessed is a departure from the righteousness of God (64:5-6).

There is really no incongruity between these companion emphases on ritual purity and righteous living. Correct ceremonial observance is never treated as meritorious in itself. The Lord's approval of those who keep the sabbath immediately follows his command to "keep justice and do righteousness" (56:1-2). Opposition to the pagan cults is linked with denunciation of adultery, harlotry, and deceit (57:3-4). The prophet was writing at a time when spiritual faith was seriously threatened by degraded forms of worship. He saw truly that ethical religion needs embodiment in forms of devotion which are harmonious with it, and therefore insisted on both, without in the slightest overlooking the distinction between them.

GOD'S WORD TO CHRISTIANS

Cannot Christians today hear the voice of God in each of the contrasts we have discussed? Certainly the Church is called to confront the nation and the world with the choice between defiance of

God, which brings destruction, and obedience to him, which leads to life. Just as clearly we are summoned to that repentance and contrition which are necessary if we and our world are to find healing and wholeness. Again, the prophet challenges us to make the Lord's house "a house of prayer for all peoples," regardless of race, color, or national origin, while warning us, by his own blind spots, how easy it is to regard people as "equal before God" while denying to them the fundamental rights which belong to all his children. Finally, these poems bid us join worship and life, combining depth of devotion with quickened response to human need, and finding in the God we meet in true worship strength for adventurous commitment.

FORTY DEVOTIONAL READINGS FROM ISAIAH

151

BOOKS ABOUT ISAIAH

Books in print may be ordered from The Methodist Publishing House serving your territory. (Prices are subject to change.) Your local church, public, and college libraries may be able to lend you books marked "out of print."

I. The Entire Book

THE ABINGDON BIBLE COMMENTARY. Edited by F. C. Eiselen, Edwin Lewis, and D. G. Downey. "Isaiah," by Robert W. Rogers, pp. 628-676. Nashville: Abingdon Press, 1929. $8.75. Indexed, $10.

ANDERSON, BERNHARD W. *Understanding the Old Testament.* New York: Prentice Hall, 1957. $7.95.

BEWER, JULIUS A. *The Book of Isaiah.* (Harper's Annotated Bible) New York: Harper & Bros., 1950. 2 vols. $.95 each.

BOX, G. H. *The Book of Isaiah.* New York: The Macmillan Co., 1909. (Out of print.)

THE INTERPRETER'S BIBLE. Edited by George A. Buttrick. Vol. V: *Ecclesiastes, Song of Songs, Isaiah, Jeremiah.* Nashville: Abingdon Press, 1956. $8.75.

KISSANE, E. J. *The Book of Isaiah.* 2 vols. Dublin: Browne and Nolan, 1941-43. (Out of print.)

KNUDSON, ALBERT C. *The Beacon Lights of Prophecy.* New York: Methodist Book Concern, 1914. (Out of print.)

LESLIE, ELMER A. *The Prophets Tell Their Own Story.* New York: Abingdon Press, 1939. $2.50.

MCFADYEN, JOHN EDGAR. *The Book of the Prophecies of Isaiah.* New York: The Macmillan Co., 1910. (Out of print.)

MILLER, MADELINE S. and J. LANE. *Harper's Bible Dictionary.* New York: Harper & Bros., 1952. pp. 284-287. $7.95.

PATERSON, JOHN. *The Goodly Fellowship of the Prophets.* New York: Charles Scribner's Sons, 1949. $3.

PFEIFFER, ROBERT H. *The Books of the Old Testament*. New York: Harper & Bros., 1957. $5.

SCOTT, R.B.Y. *The Relevance of the Prophets*. New York: The Macmillan Co., 1954. $3.

SKINNER, JOHN. *The Book of Isaiah*. ("Cambridge Bible for Schools and Colleges.") Rev. ed. Cambridge University Press, 1915-17. 2 vols. $2.50 each.

SMITH, GEORGE ADAM. *The Book of Isaiah*. ("Expositor's Bible.") Harper & Bros., 1927. 2 vols. $2.25 each.

SMITH, J. M. P. *The Prophets and Their Times*. 2nd ed. rev. William A. Irwin. Chicago: University of Chicago Press, 1941. $4.50.

WADE, G. W. *The Book of the Prophet Isaiah*. ("Westminster Commentaries.") 2nd ed. London: Methuen & Co., 1929. 2 vols. (Out of print.)

WHITEHOUSE, OWEN C. *Isaiah*. ("New Century Bible.") New York: Oxford University Press, 1905-09. 2 vols. (Out of print.)

2. Isaiah 1-39

GRAY, G. B. *A Critical and Exegetical Commentary on the Book of Isaiah I-XXXIX*. ("International Critical Commentary.") New York: Charles Scribner's Sons, 1912. Vol 1. (Out of print.)

JEFFERSON, CHARLES E. *The Cardinal Ideas of Isaiah*. New York: The Macmillan Co., 1925. (Out of print.)

3. Isaiah 40-66

BUBER, MARTIN. *The Prophetic Faith*. New York: The Macmillan Co., 1949. $3.75.

LEVY, REUBEN. *Deutero-Isaiah*. London: Oxford University Press, 1925. (Out of print.)

NORTH, C. R. *Isaiah 40-55*. ("Torch Bible Commentaries.") London: Student Christian Movement Press, 1952. $2.25.

NORTH, C. R. *The Suffering Servant in Deutero-Isaiah*. Rev. ed. London: Oxford University Press, 1950. $4.

ROBINSON, H. WHEELER. *The Cross in the Old Testament.* Philadelphia: Westminster Press, 1955 (Includes the author's *The Cross of the Servant.* London: S. C. M. Press, 1926). $3.

ROWLEY, H. H. *The Servant of the Lord.* Napierville, Ill.: Alec. R. Allenson, 1952. $5.

SCHERER, PAUL. *Event in Eternity.* New York: Harper & Bros., 1945. $2.50.

SIMON, ULRICH. *A Theology of Salvation: A Commentary on Isaiah 40-55.* New York: The Macmillan Co., 1953. $5.

THOMAS, M. M., and CONVERSE, PAUL E. *Revolution and Redemption.*[1] New York: Friendship Press, 1955. $.60.

TORREY, C. C. *The Second Isaiah.* New York: Charles Scribner's Sons, 1928. $5.

SUPPLEMENTARY MATERIALS

GUIDE TO *Isaiah Speaks*[1] by Estelle Darsey Dameron.

DRAMA *Behold Your God*[1] by Faye W. Brownfield.

MAP "The Divided Kingdom".[1] 35c.

BURROWS, MILLAR. *The Dead Sea Scrolls.* New York: Viking Press, 1955. $6.50.

FINEGAN, JACK. *Wanderer upon Earth.* New York: Harper & Bros., 1956. $3.75.

KRAELING, EMIL G. *Rand McNally Bible Atlas.* New York: Rand McNally, 1957. $8.95.

WRIGHT, GEORGE ERNEST and FILSON, FLOYD VIVIAN, (eds.). *The Westminster Historical Atlas to the Bible.* Rev. ed. Philadelphia: Westminster Press, 1956. $7.50.

A good record album of Handel's oratorio, *The Messiah.*

[1]Order from Literature Headquarters, Woman's Division
of Christian Service, 7820 Reading Road, Cincinnati 37, Ohio.

WOMAN'S DIVISION OF CHRISTIAN SERVICE
BOARD OF MISSIONS, THE METHODIST CHURCH
LITERATURE HEADQUARTERS, 7820 READING ROAD,
CINCINNATI 37, OHIO

2/58   *Price,* 75 cents